SILENT SISTERHOOD

SILENT SISTERHOOD

MIDDLE CLASS WOMEN IN THE VICTORIAN HOME

PATRICIA BRANCA

CROOM HELM LONDON

Croom Helm Ltd. 2-10 St. John's Road,
London SW11

ISBN: 0-85664-202-9

Printed by Redwood Burn Ltd.
Trowbridge and Esher

CONTENTS

TABLES

GRAPHS

ACKNOWLEDGEMENTS

I wish to thank Professors John W. Osborne, Henry R. Winkler and
Harold Perkin for their reading of the manuscript and helpful suggestions.
Professor Theresa McBride assisted in a host of ways but particularly in
her ability to discuss many of the key concepts involved.
I wish also to expres my appreciation to David Croom whose efficiency
and advice has added to the pleasure of publishing. My special thanks
goes to Professor Peter Nathaniel Stearns who gave me, and continues
to give me, sound advice, solid criticism and devoted encouragement;
without him the book would not have been.

To Nancy Ann, who endured the writing of this book nobly and who teaches me more and more what it is to be a middle class mother.

PART I
THE OUTER WOMAN

1 THE VICTORIAN WOMAN – OFF THE PEDESTAL AND INTO HISTORY

The middle-class woman in the Victorian period was a new phenomenon, in a sense the first modernized woman. Her social situation was certainly new, in that she was part of the rising middle class of the nineteenth century – the urban, professional and business class. Her working-class counterpart, also new to industrial urban life, played a vital role as well, but she strove as much as possible to preserve the traditional family structure during most of the century[1]. Traditionalism played an important part in the middle-class woman's life also, but on the whole her functions were new, for she had to mediate many of the changes that developed as the family moved into the urban middle class. In economic terms, she was responsible for much of the early transformation of the family from a unit of production to a unit of consumption. Yet, despite her novelty, the Victorian woman has not been directly studied – often characterized, but never closely examined.

Modernization is an admittedly vague term, and its application to women's history is new. We will develop a fuller outline of the applicability of the concept after we have established the areas of life in which modernizing change can be seen to occur. For in seemingly prosaic activities such as the running of the household or care of personal health women were coming to believe in change, in the relevance of new technology, and in the desirability and possibility of improved well-being. Albeit within a family context, they were coming to think of themselves as individuals. All of which fits the general modernization model, and justifies the nineteenth century as the era in which to seek the bases of the emergence of the modern woman. This is not of course to imply that previous centuries were stagnant. We know that in many respects British economic practices and politics had departed from purely traditional models long before industrialization began. We have been recently reminded that some popular values, relating even more closely to women, might change as well. But there is little evidence that the world from which middle-class women emerged had been greatly altered by forces of modernization prior to the nineteenth century. At the top of society, eighteenth-century salons had little effect in spreading new ideas to this middle sector; while changes influencing lower-class behavior definitely stopped once one reached the property-owning classes from which the new middle class would come.[2] However the traditionalist tone of most literature available to new middle-class women well into the nineteenth century, the evidence of continued traditional behavior (as in birth rates and marriage ages) suggests that

1

pre-industrial modernization in other sectors had not deeply touched the women in what was to become the new middle class. Hence our use of the terms 'modern' and 'traditional,' to describe a transitional period that might seem belated if applied to other groups (principally male) and forms of activity in Britain. Hence also the high probability that modernization as a process involved women with greater suddenness than was the case with men, causing confusion, sometimes even despair, in a group whose material circumstances might seem to assure relative flexibility in response to change. Long sheltered by the domestic circle from strangeness and change,[3] women now faced change with a vengeance, possibly carried further from tradition in the modernization process than was the case with men.[4] It is precisely toward the middle of the nineteenth century, after symptoms of modernity were well-established, such as urbanization and commercialization, that we can begin to capture the distinctive female response.

The discussion thus centres on the period between 1830 and 1880, when the new middle class rapidly expanded its ranks. From 1803 to 1867, when precise data are available, its rate of increase was 223 per cent compared to the 206 per cent growth for the general population.[5] The mid-century decades saw not only the development of the Victorian woman, as the product of a particular age, but also the beginnings of more enduring changes in the woman's situation. We are dealing, in other words, both with a distinctive historical type and with the transition to the first modern woman.

To be sure, the term Victorian can be chronologically misleading. It has been shown quite convincingly that "Victorianism" began well before 1837, the year the Queen, who gave her name to the age, assumed the throne.[6] The association of this period with the stodgy, old, black-draped queen is regrettable, especially for the women of the period. The Victorian Age was a dynamic age, and this study deals principally with the theme of change. Among the important developments which profoundly altered the life of the middle-class woman were industrialization, urbanization, and the impact of science. For the majority of women in this study there were traumatic changes associated with moving from the rural and lower classes into the urban and middle class. Too many of our images of Victorian women assume a settled state, a complacency, whereas in reality the dominant problem was assimilation to a very new life style.

Married women were chosen as the subject of this study because marriage provided the most typical role for the middle-class woman in the nineteenth century. There has been some tendency to focus on the plight of the single girl, as if her situation became increasingly important for women's history. If anything, this only reflects urbanization, which partially disrupted traditional functions for the single woman; it does

2

not represent a real statistical change. Marriage still constituted the normal pattern of life for most women – indeed for a higher percentage than in earlier centuries. Admittedly the clearest figures apply to the general population and not the middle class specifically, but the following table on the marital status of women from 1851-1901 demonstrates the overall pattern.

TABLE I

Proportions of Unmarried, Married, and Widowed in 1000 Females In Various Age Groups

Age and Condition As to Marriage		Years 1851	1861	1871	1881	1891	1901
15 to 20	Unmarried	974	970	968	975	981	985
	Married	25	30	32	25	19	15
	Widowed	0	0	0	0	0	0
20 to 25	Unmarried	687	664	652	665	701	726
	Married	308	331	343	331	296	272
	Widowed	28	28	30	26	21	17
25 to 35	Unmarried	329	305	294	293	326	340
	Married	643	667	676	681	653	643
	Widowed	28	28	30	26	21	17
35 to 45	Unmarried	163	159	156	153	164	185
	Married	757	762	762	765	761	751
	Widowed	80	79	82	82	75	64
45 to 55	Unmarried	122	119	120	119	124	136
	Married	716	720	717	711	706	705
	Widowed	162	161	163	170	170	159
55 to 65	Unmarried	115	109	109	109	110	117
	Married	589	589	589	581	573	569
	Widowed	296	302	302	310	317	314

Source: *Census of England and Wales, 1911*, General Report, Table XXI, p. 90.

Marriage frequency did not change fundamentally in the second half of the nineteenth century, as the previous table confirms. Professor D.V. Glass has made the same observation, reporting that in 1850-52 out of 1000 girls who were unmarried at the age of 15, 859 could expect to have married at least once by the time they reached their 50th birthday.

In 1860-62, the probability was 848 in 1000. In 1870-72, it was 866. The census data for the years 1881-1901 did not allow for a comparably accurate computation but in 1910-12 the rate was still relatively similar at 818.[7] Thus the plight of single girls, though it may have become more visible with urbanization, did not rest on a dramatic demographic increase relative to the whole population. And certainly the history of women becomes distorted if it focuses primarily on this group.

However, it has been claimed that the situation of single women in the middle class was both particularly anguished and extremely common. The statistical basis for this latter claim is very shaky; one author holds that twenty-five out of every hundred women lacked husbands during the second half of the century,[8] which is doubtful in view of the general demographic evidence cited above. But because of the lack of class-specific statistical data, a problem we will encounter throughout much of this study, it is impossible to refute this claim precisely. Nevertheless, there is little reason to believe that the middle-class woman's marriage opportunities differed so drastically from those of the general female population, save that they may have been better than average. It has been noted that the opportunities for marriage were greatly increased with urbanization.[9] The middle-class woman was an important part of the urban community. There were not any obvious professional fields to which the middle-class woman was flocking as an alternative to marriage. Indeed some occupations that might have provided suitable if degrading employment for unmarried middle-class women, such as governesses, in fact encountered a lack of suitable candidates. It might indeed be suggested that the middle-class woman was a better marriage choice than the lower-class woman, for she could serve as an upward mobility channel for an ambitious lower-class male. A minority of servant and working-class spinsters, plus some remnants of lower traditional rural marriage rates account for a disproportionate percentage of the permanently unmarried women; the middle class contributed unusually fully in the general increase in marriage rates during the century as a whole.[10]

Some of the confusion surrounding the middle-class woman's marriage pattern no doubt arises from the postponement of marriage controversy. It has been traditionally accepted that in the second half of the nineteenth century, the rising cost of living was forcing many middle-class men to postpone marriage.[11] The evidence for this assumption is not totally clear, for the groups cited as postponing marriage, that is the clerical, legal and medical professions, have always married at a later age.[12] Nevertheless, there is no reason to assume that later age in age of marriage for the male necessarily correlates with a decline in the marriage opportunities for the middle-class female.[13] On the whole, middle-class women married at age 25, which was at most one to three years older than the age of the general female population at marriage which ranged between 20 and 24.

Thus it seems imperative that for a study of middle-class women in the nineteenth century, we focus our attention on the situation of the married woman as being most representative of the middle-class woman's life style. Most middle-class women spent their entire lives first in their mother's home till age 25, and then in their own home until their death. This study, by concentrating on the domestic life of middle-class women, is intended not only to contribute substantially to our understanding of the middle-class woman but also to add to our understanding of the Victorian family. Despite the frequent emphasis on the importance of home and family for Victorian England, particularly for the middle class,[14] there are a host of open questions still. Above all, the middle-class family has been more often stereotyped than studied, and this contrast provides the first step in the present investigation.

For it might seem redundant to offer another study of the Victorian woman, given the fact that there has been no other woman in history who has attracted so much interest. In the last few years her appeal has reached new heights. Books on this most colorful and controversial woman flood the market. Among the more recent are Duncan Crow's *The Victorian Woman*[15] and Martha Vicinus's collection of essays, *Suffer and Be Still.*[16] No doubt the violent explosion of the women's liberation movement in recent times has added to the popularity of this woman, for indeed she did give birth to the movement in its first modern stage.

The increasing interest in social history has contributed to the new surge of books on women. However, the overall effect, to date, has not been too fruitful. Simply dealing with the subject of women does not automatically make one a social historian. Many of the so-called social histories of women are merely second-rate journalistic attempts to exploit a lucrative market. In order to broaden their appeal, and thereby increase their returns, they are written for shock value rather than as serious studies; for example Crow's *The Victorian Woman* and Pearsall's *The Worm in the Bud,*[17] both of which heavily exploit the sex interests of the general public. In fact, none of the existing studies of the middle-class woman is based on more than individual images and impressions; none attempts to deal with middle-class women as a generally inarticulate segment of a large social class, or with the immense difficulties in source materials that this topic involves.

The portrait all too many of the studies paint of the Victorian woman is not only incomplete — that is inevitable in the circumstances — but is a picture reflected in a distorted mirror. This essay I hope will be different. It is not about "eminent women", the women of British country house parties, or even the women in the drawing room "at home" among the leisured classes. It is not about the superstars – the Florence Nightingales and the Josephine Butlers. It is not about the militant suffragettes. It is about ordinary middle-class women. One of the purposes of this book will be to rescue the Victorian middle-class woman from the realm of myth which has so long surrounded her and bring her into the light of reality.

In general, historians have viewed the Victorian middle-class woman's role in society as merely ornamental rather than functional or responsible.[18] Disparaging images besiege her.She is often depicted as the "doll-like, bread and butter miss swooning on a sofa," the frivolous, irrational, irresponsible creature of whim, the devotee of fashion, and of course, "the virgin-in-the-drawing-room,"[19] the strait-laced, thin-lipped prude, who blushed at such suggestive words as 'legs.' With these stereotypes predominating, her life has been dismissed as a 'mass of trifles.'[20]

One reason for these pejorative images is that too often Victorian culture and Victorian family life have been written about by its critics. And the Victorian woman has either received the brunt of the criticism or has been the object of a patronizing sympathy, as the helpless and insipid creature of men who needed to render her functionless to rescue their own egos. Thus it is particularly the role of the woman in the family – the subject of this study – that has been most commonly belittled.

The story of the Victorian woman, so often retold, is as follows. In the early years of the century, the middle-class housewife was a very active participant in the family, fulfilling vital tasks in the dairy, the confectionery, the store-room,the still-room, the poultry garden and the kitchen. She even helped her husband with his business. She was truly the 'helpmeet' of her husband. Her most important task was that of bearing children, and she was a loving and attentive mother. The tale goes on that as the century progressed more and more people prospered, especially the middle class. This new prosperity brought about significant changes in the middle-class life style, for the drive for social esteem became an obsession. The middle-class expressed this drive by acquiring what has become known as the 'paraphernalia of gentility,' large and expensive houses, elegant horses and carriages, a retinue of servants, and elaborate and lavish dinner parties. The 'Perfect Lady' was a very important element of the 'paraphernalia of gentility.' This new image brought about dramatic and direct changes in the life style of the middle-class woman.[21]

Middle-class parents, in their desire to imitate the upper classes, sent their daughters off to boarding schools where they were to acquire the elegant accomplishments necessary to becoming the 'Perfect Lady' – a little French, some music, dancing, fancy needlework, and of course, all the rules of proper etiquette. The middle-class woman no longer concerned herself with household affairs, for these duties were associated with those lower than she. Her domestic duties were limited to merely supervising and complaining about her servants.[22]

She still maintained the important function of childbearing, but this too changed considerably. It appears that the Perfect Lady not only developed a disdain for household affairs but also for sex. This was apparent in the new attitude expressed toward conception, which became an 'Eleusinian mystery'. Ideally, the Perfect Lady was to produce children by 'parthenogenesis'; failing that, male impregnation was to take place in a dark bedroom into which the husband crept to create his offspring in silence while the wife endured the connection in a sort of coma.[23] After the birth, the middle-class mother had little time for her children. They were given over to wet-nurses, nannies and governesses. A woman was considered to have done her duty to her children if she saw that they were fed, clothed and well supplied with toys.[24] The Perfect Lady was only mother at set times of the day, and then only if it was convenient for her.

The Victorian wife was still considered the 'helpmeet' of her husband but this image necessarily had to change. As the middle-class man achieved his position in the cruel, harsh, competitive outside world, he sought refuge in his home, which became his sanctuary. As her husband's 'helpmeet,' the Victorian wife was to provide the proper environment of respectability. She became the guardian of morality, the citadel of respectability. 'Helpmeet' to her husband required that she be righteous, gentle, sympathetic, and most of all submissive.[25] This image, combined with the traditional sanctions of religion and law, insured the inferior relationship of the wife to the husband.

Strong male supremacy has long been assumed in characterizations of the Victorian family. For middle-class wives, it is often noted that 'the Pauline injunction was absolute . . . for the husband is the head of the wife, as Christ is the head of the Church.'[26] The inferior position of the wife has been demonstrated often by outlining her legal situation. Her position was that of '*feme covert* [sic], — my wife and I are one and I am he.'[27] A 'married woman' indicated a woman who had no existence in common law apart from the husband. The double standard in the law is very familiar, as it is a popular subject with the feminists. Among the Victorian woman's legal disabilities was the fact that she could not give testimony in court, nor sue in court without her husband's name. A husband could enforce his right to his wife's consortium by attachment of person, and could force her to return to him. A divorce was very costly and only obtainable through an Act of Parliament. Adultery was the only cause needed for a divorce when sought by a husband but a wife had to prove an additional charge — either cruelty, desertion, bigamy, incest, rape, sodomy, or bestiality. A woman had no legal right to her children.[28]

The woman's economic dependency was just as complete. She did not work, and even if she did, her earnings belonged to her husband. He had complete right to any property or money she earned or inherited. The effects of this complete inferiority according to the common view were not beneficial. Because the middle-class woman was given little responsibility for administering or organizing in the family, she was often considered untrustworthy. The rarified moral atmosphere in which she lived made her unrealistic.[29]

This image of the useless, idle female goes well beyond her exterior behavior. It is also part of her inner being. Interest in Victorian middle-class women's health is just beginning to elicit new interest. According to recent historians her health condition reflected her inferior position in society;[30] she was a weak frail creature with a poor constitution. The majority suffered from depression, headaches, listlessness and hysteria — or what has been termed the 'fashionable diseases.' The Victorian woman, plagued by these nervous afflictions, indulged her suffering spirits to extravagant rest cures and water cures.

However, as noted earlier, our perspective on the middle-class family has been distorted by those who seek to profit by portraying the Victorian woman as an odd museum piece — indeed it is odd that such should prove commercially interesting to the reading public — or by playing up the titillating aspects of Victorian subculture. For example, a discussion of women in the nineteenth century inevitably leads to a discussion of prostitution, so that at times one gets the impression that prostitution was unique to Victorian society and a vital counterpart to the sexless Victorian female.[31]

Unfortunately, distortion also arises from the works of the feminists. In their efforts to rectify the injustices of the society, they have tended to focus solely on the inequities and those who have sought to remedy them. However, in doing this, they have oddly downgraded the real situation and ignored the actual struggle of the women they seek to portray; for example, the women who were not Florence Nightingales or Josephine Butlers tend to appear less worthy because they did not rebel in any visible or vocal manner. A simple example of the distortion which inadvertently arises from the feminists' works is found in the above discussion of the double standard in the law. Indeed the inequities were, in theory, real and in need of reform. Few, however, have acknowledged that it was in this Victorian society that the inequities were beginning to be rectified. Among the changes was the Infant Custody Act of 1839, which gave mothers the custody of their children under seven, with the right of access to their older children at stated times. By mid-century divorce became more accessible to the middle-class woman with Matrimonial Cause Act of 1857 which created a new court and made the procedure less expensive. In 1878, maintenance was made available to the wife. Legislation further rectifying the inequities of divorce proceedings followed in 1884, 1886 and 1895. In 1870, the Married Woman's Property Act gave the woman the right to own property for her own use and entitled her to all wages she earned. This act was expanded and made more effective in 1882. Surely it is worth asking whether these legal changes stemmed from prior developments in family relationships, as well as examining their impact. Law is at best a vague description of society, and the changes were more probably predicated on the real social situation than on the inferiorities. The reality of the situation is that many of the legal rights of the husband were merely theoretical and never exercised in the great majority of middle-class homes. Other laws did indeed relate to the framework of middle-class life, but in no sense dominated day-to-day life. Divorce, for example, was not considered an alternative for most middle-class women, who also had neither earnings nor property to protect. Attention to laws on these matters is not irrelevant, but can distract from understanding the actual life situation.

A more subtle problem arises with the feminists' treatment of women's health conditions. Discussion of Victorian nervous disorders, on the lines noted earlier, leads logically into a condemnation of male doctors who manipulated them. But it has been impossible to avoid characterizing these same women as docile dupes — else why did they subject themselves to misogynistic doctors at all? The fact is that real health conditions have been ignored in favor of dramatic generalizations.

This is not to imply that women did not suffer from the inequities of the society. No doubt there were husbands who ruled their domiciles in despotic fashion. No doubt there were women who were bored by a life that gave them very little to do. But how many were? Were these the most important problems faced by the middle-class housewife in the nineteenth century? One cannot answer these questions until one investigates the woman's role in the family.

Before undertaking this investigation, it is necessary to discuss two problems facing anyone who studies the history of women — the problems of methodology and sources. The study of women does not lend itself to the traditional historical approaches. Since women did not possess political power, they are invisible in the political field. Since they also had no legal voice, they have been ignored by the political historians at least until the rise of the suffragettes. Since they lacked sufficient economic power to exert any influence, they have been obscured in the studies of economic history. The working-class woman, in contrast to the middle-class woman, has received a little more substantial treatment; for example, the classic works of Ivy Pinchbeck's *Women Workers in the Industrial Revolution*,[32] Wanda F. Nef's

Victorian Working Women[33] and closest to a social history of working women, Margaret Hewitt's *Wives and Mothers in Victorian Industry*.[34] This is due in part to the fact that these women played a visible role in the labor force, although ironically the fact that most working-class women did not, and have therefore been ignored by the historians of the class, is only now becoming widely recognized.[35]

Middle-class women, who remained in the home even more commonly, have escaped social historians altogether. Only a few approaches have been attempted. C. Willett Cunnington seeks to describe Victorian women through a study of their dress, finding fashion in dress woman's only means of self-expression.[36] The psychological implications that he derives from the type of clothing women wore are indeed fascinating but their usefulness in describing the average middle-class woman is questionable. For fashion as a source turns out to be high fashion, which has understandably left the best records, but which does not at all typify the middle-class life style.

Other historical accounts have relied heavily upon biographical studies of a few eminent women.[37] This approach again produces useful data but it is inherently limited in that these women have made their mark in history precisely because they were unusual. It is hazardous indeed to relate the experiences of a few individual women to that of the average woman of the day.

The most popular approach, to date, especially for studies of 'Victorian women' in some collective sense, consists of the study of the political struggle of women.[38] This approach is employed so often not only because of its political attractiveness but because it relies on a traditional historical method. But it leads to obvious distortion. The over emphasis on the English feminist movement is understandable, for this was the first vocal and visible outcry by middle-class women. But it tends also to summarize the bulk of the Victorian period as a mere staging area for the inevitable political explosion. Here the method is particularly wanting, for it was not until the late '80s and '90s that the feminist movement began to gain any widespread support in England. One naturally wonders that Victorian women were doing before this; surely they were not merely planning for a final outburst.

The feminist studies and many of the biographical studies are closely related to the pedestal image of the idle Victorian woman. This, rather than any desire to pick at historians who have at least recognized women as a legitimate historical topic, necessitates these preliminary remarks on existing methodology. Almost all the studies on Victorian women have one theme in common — the theme of discontent. It is the generally accepted position that more and more women, bored with their life of genteel uselessness, sought more meaningful roles outside the home. In other words, the feminist movement was a reaction against boredom,[39] while the eminent women achieved their position by defying the common norms. And here of course is the interpretative problem: feminism and the eminent women alike may fit our standards of significance, but they almost by definition depart from the situation, if not the values, of middle-class women during most of the nineteenth century. It is possible that we will learn more even about recent women's history by studying the typical situation than by studying the departures therefrom.

For in fact the history of women is, or ought to be, the history of the inarticulate. There exists a genuine need to hear from the multitudes of mute inglorious females of whom no biography was ever written, who never did or said or thought a thing that would distinguish them from the mass of women of the day. Of course, the great problem is lack of sources. Biographies are written because a few individuals left material behind them. The same holds for the histories of the feminist movement, for this movement is easy to investigate because the material is readily available, abundant and articulate.

The real lack of autobiographical data describing the life history of the 'typical' middle-class female has caused many studies to rely heavily upon the fiction of the day.[40] These sources have contributed greatly to the image of the completely leisured, ornamental, helpless and dependent female with no other function in society besides inspiring admiration and bearing children. The ladies in Miss Austen's novels are a case in point, for they had little to do but to read poetry, relate local gossip, and await the attention of gentlemen. In other novels, Rosamond Vincy and Dora Spenlow are portrayed as women skilled in elaborate feminine delicacy and aloof from domestic duties. The works of the nineteenth-century novelists, such as Jane Austen, Charles Dickens, and William Thackeray are familiar and popular today. But we tend to forget that they were first and foremost story-tellers and not social historians. Peter Laslett's caution against the novels, in *The World We Have Lost,* is worth repeating. He noted that

> . . . it is indeed hazardous to infer an institution or a habit characteristic of a whole society or a whole era from the central character of a literary work and its story, from *Pamela*, for example, or from Elizabeth Bennet in *Pride and Prejudice* . . . The outcome may be to make people believe that what was the entirely exceptional, was in fact the perfectly normal.[41]

This is indeed what has happened to the Victorian woman.

Because of the many problems in interpretation, this study does not rely upon novels. It does not depend on the literature of the feminists, nor on biographical studies of eminent women. This is not to suggest that these sources should be completely neglected in an ultimate

11

assessment; but they do not constitute the most direct approach to the middle-class woman and can be properly utilized only after a more relevant framework is established. Instead, we will rely on totally different sources, and above all material that was written especially for the English housewife. For nineteenth-century England there is an overwhelming amount of printed material of this sort in the forms of household manuals, women's magazines, health manuals, marriage manuals, child care manuals and family magazines. These sources were written by and for the middle class, as indicated in a number of their prefaces. One typical manual noted in its preface that

> . . . it is chiefly for THEM that we have undertaken our task, to
> unite elegance with economy, not only in the highest, but
> in the middle walks of life, and to show that good old
> English housewifery is still a good old English Virtue.[42]

Another author defined her readership as 'those women who belong to that great mass of the population of England which is connected with trade and manufacture, as well as to wives and daughters of professional men of limited income . . . .'[43]

Obviously it would have been impossible and somewhat futile to consult every book and periodical written for women. Some selectivity was needed for practical reasons. Those sources which applied directly to her problems in the home and particularly household management, budgeting, servants, children, and health were used extensively. The many books on etiquette, fashion, and entertainment were not used as much because they were generally too superficial. Indeed, as has already been implied, and will be clarified in a later chapter, these books are misleading precisely because they described a life style far too expensive for the middle class.

The use of the various middle-class manuals is not new. Some of the classical works examined in this study, such as the books by Mrs. Ellis[44] and Mrs. Beeton,[45] have often been quoted elsewhere. Here, however, the effort was more comprehensive, and particular attention was paid to the manuals which dealt with the problems of people on limited incomes. This creates a certain tension, which will be more fully explored in the next chapter, between manuals that were demonstrably closer to the actual middle-class life style and those which may have been more popular. What we have is a large sample of the material that dealt with various aspects of the housewife's daily life including all the best-sellers — and some material found a wide middle-class market. The first section, which deals with the household manuals most directly, consists essentially of a study in popular culture, defined simply as values widely disseminated among a middle-class audience, and here we can clearly indicate what sentiments are typical of the manual literature and what are out of line. The ultimate aim is to go beyond this approach,

12

because the tone of the popular manuals could be misleading, but we can at least begin with the careful survey of the books and pamphlets that were most directly relevant to the housewife's concerns.

Nineteenth-century England produced an amazing number of authorities on household management; and there were several different approaches in the books of household advice. One approach was that of a dialogue between the author, 'A Lady,' the perfect housekeeper, and the inexperienced wife, the congenital idiot who was presumably anxious to have her mistakes corrected. Mrs. Eliza Warren's popular works, such as *How I Managed My House on Two Hundred Pounds a Year*[46] (which sold 36,000 copies in its first year) and *How I Managed My Children From Infancy to Marriage*[47] (sold 20,000 copies) were typical of this approach. So al o was Alexis Soyer's *The Modern Housewife or Ménagère*,[48] which was published in 1849 and sold 30,000 by 1857.

Another popular approach, rather closely related to the first, was the straightforward monologue of words of wisdom from a mature housekeeper who placed before the young wife all the rules that she needed to know for ordering her life. The emphasis in this type of book of advice was more on social behavior in the abstract rather than practical problems of everyday life. But it is useful because it represented what the woman's position was supposed to be. Typical of this approach were the works of the very prolific Mrs. Sarah Strickney Ellis, whose more popular works included *The Women of England*, *The Daughters of England*, and *The Mothers of England.*[49]

The third approach, which became extremely successful in the second half of the century and was soon to lead the market in books on household management, was the scientific approach. The great benefit of this newer type of source was their claim to combine the advances of science with the practices of the day, thereby hopefully insuring the proper and efficient running of the home. Some of the books which purported to use this method were John Walsh's *A Manual of Domestic Economy: Suited to Families Spending from £100 to £1000 a Year*[50] and, of course, the now classic work of Mrs. Beeton, *The Book of Household Management*,[51] which sold 30,000 copies in three years.

These sources were valuable because they contained a wide variety of information on almost every aspect of domestic life. They provided information on marketing, keeping of stores, furnishing, cooking, carving, cleaning, and dealing with 'insult of no pleasing description', on conduct to be observed toward former friends, the choice of new acquaintances, and how to deal with one's mother-in-law. There was sometimes a section on the law concerning purchasing of a house and rental contracts. There was usually a section on medical advice,

13

including the care and feeding of infants and invalids and what to do in an emergency. Sometimes the most important information was not easy to uncover; for example, in *The Household Book of Domestic Economy*, one found on a single page directions for stewed tomatoes, dealing with depression of the spirits, suggestions on treatment for epilepsy, a method of cleaning rose trees from blight and also directions on how to roast a hare.[52]

The market for women's magazines was first realized in the nineteenth century, but it was in the second half of the century that it was fully exploited. One of the most popular journals was *The Englishwoman's Domestic Magazine*, first published in 1852. By 1861, it had over 60,000 readers.[53] In addition to the women's magazines, there were the more general family and home periodicals, such as *The Family Friend*, which first appeared in 1847. In ten years it distributed 4,800,000 copies and received 520,000 letters from its readers.[54] These letters to the editor were especially valuable, for they constitute one of the few times these 'inarticulate' women spoke. The advertisements of the magazines were helpful also in that they reflected the tastes, and often the costs, of the middle-class life style.

An especially valuable source for this study of women was the health manual. These manuals became increasingly popular in the second half of the century. They were often written by medical men and thus indicated the advances and impact of science on society; common problems encountered by the Victorian woman as wife and mother were dealt with in a more intimate manner than in the general household manuals. The health manuals constitute on the whole a more valuable source, for they talk more directly of the actual concerns and anxieties of the middle-class woman. They will thus be used in a different fashion from the household manuals, and in a different section. In addition to health manuals, medical journals and treatises of the nineteenth century were used in order to determine the condition of health of the woman and the methods of treatment extended to her.

These sources taken together offer a more significant and representative image of the middle-class woman than the literature explored to date because they deal with the daily activities of the average housewife. However, these sources have a series of limitations. The greatest problem was in trying to determine, in this cornucopia of sources on the home and family, what was representative of the average middle-class life style. Obviously, books written for the middle class, even if widely read by a significant minority, do not necessarily reflect uniformly held views; inevitably there would be a gap between probability and proof. But in fact the problem is even larger than this, and contributes in an unexpected way to an understanding of the dilemma of the middle-class woman. Many of the household manuals were predominantly cook-books and probably sold for that reason alone; yet it is tempting to use their more general advice to illustrate the household situation of the middle-class woman. Here is the problem of representativeness writ large, for quite apart from the vagaries of the author the purpose of purchase may have been quite remote from the material the historians wish to interpret. (Mrs. Beeton's manual, for example, was especially attractive because it added color plates to its edition, which made it a nice gift item for newly-weds, and probably accounts for its popularity more than anything it said about the middle-class life style.) In terms of the stereotypes of Victorian women, it may prove as important to realize that they actually cooked, and therefore needed cook-books, as to go through the varied recommendations of the manuals on other aspects of life.

For it is possible to use the manuals to confirm many of the stereotypes of the Victorian woman. The one study that has used this source extensively does just this, for the findings of Professor A. Banks, in his book *Prosperity and Parenthood*, largely corroborate the image of the idle Victorian woman. Banks was the first to develop fully the concepts of 'paraphernalia of gentility' and the 'Perfect Lady' as important characteristics of middle-class life style. His findings have since been quoted in book after book as the last word on the middle class in the nineteenth century.[55] However, Banks himself noted that his work was a pioneer study and his findings only tentative. There was nothing sacrosanct about his choice of sources, which merely appeared to him at the time to be representative.

But what Banks intended as tentative, in a genuinely pioneering effort to get at a vital topic in the history of women, has been taken as the final word, so that impressionistic overtones derived from a limited body of material continue to describe Victorian women's behavior, as cited not just by women's historians *per se* but by demographers and others dealing with vital social developments that can so simply be explained by leaving the woman on her powerless pedestal, or even inching her up a notch or two.

How can we claim to improve on this approach? We want more than impressions; we claim more than simply another subjective view of conventional material. Because our primary concern is with changes in mentalities, and because our subjects were normally inarticulate, not, even mounting sporadic protest which might be taken as indicative of widely-held attitudes, we cannot advance definitive conclusions in every case. But we can presume to present a fuller and, at key points, unexpected picture of middle-class women for the following reasons. Manuals and related literature addressed to these women were investigated more systematically than has been the practice heretofore. This means reading advertisements and letters to the editor, often at least as seriously as the hortative advice which itself may contradict our image of perfect ladyship. Second, a wider range of manual literature was consulted, some of it more directly relevant to real middle-class life than the materials that have attracted attention to date. And this in turn involves use of other material about actual behavior, which gives us some basis for checking the relevance of any kind of manual to middle-class life and values and allows us to discriminate between ideals that were known but not taken too seriously, and attitudes that shaped an actual style of life.

The diverse uses to which a given manual can be put will be illustrated at many points in what follows. The variety within the literature itself deserves more explicit introductory comment, for here we need only to look at two of the more popular works — the book by Mrs. Warren[56] and that by Mrs. Beeton[57] — to begin to suggest how one can judge the representativeness of this kind of source. Among the students of Victorian society, Mrs. Beeton has come to be known as the mentor of the middle-class housewife. Her work is most often quoted as representative of middle class. According to Mrs. Beeton's advice to the English housewife, it does appear that the Victorian woman spent most of her time in idle leisure. Her main duties were supervising the servants, seeing that the children were properly attended to by the nurse, making and receiving calls from her friends, and attending or giving lavish dinner parties. However, Mrs. Warren presented another side of the English housewife's life. According to Mrs. Warren, the average day of the mistress of the house was filled with housework, washing, cooking, crying children, quarrels with the maid, shopping, and never-ending financial problems. Both women claimed to be speaking to the middle-class housewife, but obviously they were not talking to the same woman. Mrs. Warren was more specific about the woman she was speaking to, for her woman lived on £200 per year. Mrs. Beeton's woman apparently lived on a higher income level. It is true that Mrs. Beeton's book was more representative of the manual literature in general, but this is precisely the problem with the source. If we take many of the manuals literally, we merely exacerbate the distortions of the middle-class woman, for the manuals reflected an upper-class life style rather than a middle-class situation. Yet by reading between the lines, and by using materials such as the Warren book, we can indicate crucial differences between the two classes. The middle-class housewife had little time to spend on morning calls, afternoon teas, and so forth; she had too much to do at home.

In other words, the manual literature takes us well beyond the study of eminent women or political unrest, but it is not enough. The fact that it was widely purchased probably indicates, as suggested above, a disparity between the prosaic interests of the readers, seeking a new recipe or pattern, and the moral intentions of the authors. Yet the unrealistic advice, so often critical of actual middle-class women, may have made its mark on the readers as well, increasing their feelings of inadequacy. And the readers' expectations may have been sufficiently out of phase with their actual situation to make a bit of unreality attractive.

Nevertheless, important as the assessment of the manuals is, it was obviously necessary to search beyond these sources. The need for a clear statistical base was most pressing. An attempt was made, even if sometimes rather arbitrary and tentative, to supply, whenever possible, a material framework for the study, and so quantitative sources were used to help define the middle-class life style. Thus this study depended on a wide variety of materials for different points of information. The sources were sometimes used to complement each other, but more often to check each other; for example, statistical data were used when available to determine how representative the literature of the household manuals was of middle-class life style. The health manuals were checked in the same fashion, and one of the reasons they can be taken as a more reliable source is because of the coincidence of their discussion with statistical evidence on disease. Also it might be suggested that the authors were more familiar with the middle class because as doctors their patients were largely from the middle class. Hence, they were able to provide a better perspective on middle-class living conditions. By using the health manuals for a description of the more intimate and personal aspects of the woman's life, plus the household manuals for a discussion of the tasks and outside forces the woman had to encounter daily, plus statistical data to quantify our image, we arrive at a better — though not yet complete — understanding of what it was like to be a middle-class woman in nineteenth-century England.

It must be recognized that for the most part the middle class, male as well as female, has remained a non-entity for nineteenth-century history, despite the existence of a few books on the subject[58] and the fact that social histories often abound with generalizations about their life style.[59] In comparison with the working-class the middle-class remains an unknown quantity.[60] This is shocking in view of the great importance which has correctly been placed on the role of the middle-class in the nineteenth century. Middle-class values and motives are often cited; for example, the entrepreneurial spirit, optimism, the belief in progress and rational decision-making are all generally considered middle-class,[61] yet no one has clearly defined what is middle-class. Income, occupation, religion, education and home style have been used as determinants, but their vagueness leaves one with an almost meaningless definition. For example, middle-class income has been defined as low as £60 per year, and as high as £1400 year.[62] In another

17

approach middle-class occupations include everything that is non-manual labor. Thus the petty clerk in a big business enterprise is considered middle class, along with the owner of the enterprise. The differences in the two life styles must indeed have been great, and in actuality historians have focused on the upper levels, revealing almost nothing about the middle and lower levels of the middle class.[63]

The problems of coming to terms with the middle class in the nineteenth century are further complicated by the lack of information on its tradition. Its tremendous rate of increase in the first half of the century indicates that its heritage must have been from the other sectors in society. What part of this new middle class was of rural origin, what part was of artisan or laboring ancestry? It is very important that we understand the traditions of the middle class because, as noted in the beginning, the prime responsibility for mediating the changes associated with urbanization and industrialization was placed upon the middle class. How they adopted and adjusted to the new changes was dependent in part on where they came from.

The problems which surround the middle-class in general are obviously enhanced for a study of middle-class women. Middle-class men, at least, were counted in census materials. They were heads of households. They paid taxes and rent and thus there is some statistical information on them, even though no one has yet sought to investigate it precisely. Housewives were never studied. The only time they were ever counted was in the 1871 census. And middle-class housewives, because they represented a small proportion of the general population, were totally obscured. The middle-class woman spent most of her time behind closed doors. No one bothered with her and she did not have the time nor interest to bother with the outside world. In contrast, the upper-class woman could be involved in activities outside the home, in the various reform movements, the charity benefits, or the social events of the day which filled the daily society columns of the many newspapers. This is the reason so much more is known of her life style. The lower-class woman who went out to work was subject to some attention also, as noted earlier. Her problems were far more visible and concentrated, and therefore stirred up concern in the rest of the community. However, the middle-class woman, because she did not border on poverty or live in the worst slum areas, because she could not afford to go to the fashionable charity ball or opening night at the opera, remained hidden from our view.

Nevertheless, even where serious questions remain, the effort to identify the middle-class woman in her role in the home represents a significant advance in approach. In order to understand the Victorian woman one must define her in her own terms. She spent most of her life in the home, and therefore we must search for her there. Her role in the family was crucial. By studying the middle-class woman's problems as mistress of the house, her problems with domestics, her problems as mother and her problems as woman we can begin not merely to characterize the middle-class woman but to define her as an element of British social history and as a silent but significant agent of change.

We start, despite their limitations, with the manuals, for even they represent a significant advance over the stereotype. They depict the woman in a meaningful and responsible position in the family. The manuals were read and deserve consideration on this basis alone. In addition to describing the everyday problems the middle-class woman had to cope with, the manuals are valuable in that they reflect the strict standards of the day, which profoundly affected the middle-class. Whether or not the Victorian woman was able to fulfill the demands of her society will be an important part of this discussion. Finally, the manuals at least indirectly suggest changes in household management, reflecting part of the new outlook toward domestic life which middle-class women quietly forged during the Victorian period.

Notes

1. Michael Anderson, *Family Structure in Nineteenth-Century Lancashire* (Cambridge, 1971).
2. See Edward Shorter, 'Female Emancipation, Birth Control and Fertility in European History,' *American Historical Review,* Vol. 78, No. 3 (June 1973), pp. 605-40, and Michael Phayer, 'Lower Class Morality: The Case of Bavaria,' *Journal of Social History*, Vol. 8, No. 1.
3. Peter Laslett, *The World We Have Lost* (New York, 1960).
4. For a discussion of the impact of modernization on women see Patricia Branca and Peter N. Stearns, *Modernization of Women in the Nineteenth Century* (Missouri, 1973).
5. For a full discussion of the growth of the middle-class see Chapter II. Percentage rates are based on figures of the central middle class found on page 27.
6. Asa Briggs, *The Making of Modern England 1783-1867* (New York, 1959), p. 422.; John W. Osborne, *The Silent Revolution* (New York, 1970), p.x.
7. D.V. Glass, 'Population and Population Movements in England and Wales, 1700 to 1850,' in *Population Policies and Movements*, D.V. Glass (ed.) (New York, 1967), p. 19.
8. O.R. McGregor, *Divorce in England, a Centenary Study* (London, 1957), p. 85.
9. Geoffrey Best, *Mid-Victorian Britain 1851-1875* (London, 1971), p. 106.
10. See Jeanne M. Peterson, 'The Victorian Governess: Status Incongruence,' in Martha Vicinus, *Suffer and Be Still* (Bloomington, 1972), and Theresa McBride, 'Social Mobility for the Lower Class: Domestic Servants in France,' *Journal of Social History*, Vol. 8, No. 1, for a discussion of the high rate of single women in service from the working class.
11. J.A. Banks, *Prosperity and Parenthood* (London, 1954), pp. 32-47.

12. C. Ansell reported in his work *On the Rate of Mortality at Early Periods of Life, the Age at Marriage, the Number of Children to a Marriage, the Length of a Generation, and other Statistics of Families in the Upper and Professional Classes* (1874) that before 1840, the average age at marriage for men in the clergy was 28. 85, after 1840 30.44; for lawyers before 1840, 28.24, after 1840, 29.54; for doctors before 1840, 28.36, after 1840, 29.48, p. 48.

13. J.A. Banks and Olive Banks in their work *Feminism and Family Planning in Victorian England* (New York, 1964) stated that one of the factors responsible for increasing the number of single women was postponement of marriage, p. 81.

14. Briggs, op. cit.; O.R. McGregor, *Divorce in England, a Centenary Study* (London, 1957).

15. Duncan Crow, *The Victorian Woman* (New York, 1971).

16. Martha Vicinus (ed.), *Suffer and Be Still: Women in the Victorian Age* (Bloomington, 1972).

17. R. Pearsall, *The Worm in the Bud: The World of Victorian Sexuality* (New York, 1969).

18. Harold Perkin, *The Origins of Modern English Society 1780-1880* (London, 1969); S.G. Checkland, *The Rise of Industrial Society in England 1815-1885* (London, 1964); J.F.C. Harrison, *The Early Victorians 1832-1851* (London, 1971); Best, op. cit.

19. Crow, op. cit., pp. 13-26.

20. Ibid., pp. 13, 38, 67.

21. For a full discussion of these concepts see Banks, op. cit., and Banks and Banks, op. cit.

22. McGregor, op. cit., p. 65.

23. Crow, op. cit., p. 25.

24. Banks and Banks, op. cit., p. 16.

25. Crow, op. cit., pp. 45-52; Banks and Banks, op. cit., pp. 58-9.

26. Harrison, op. cit., p. 115; McGregor, op. cit., p. 79.

27. Crow, op. cit., p. 147.

28. McGregor, op. cit., *passim.*

29. Lenore Davidoff, *The Employment of Married Women in England* (unpublished M.A. thesis, University of London, 1956), p. 290.

30. Ann Wood, 'The Fashionable Diseases: Women's Complaints and their Treatment in Nineteenth Century America,' *Journal of Interdisciplinary History* (1973).

31. Crow, op. cit., pp. 210-13; Pearsall, op. cit.

32. Ivy Pinchbeck, *Women Workers in the Industrial Revolution* (London, 1930).

33. Wanda F. Nef, *Victorian Working Women* (London, 1929).

34. Margaret Hewitt, *Wives and Mothers in Victorian Industry* (London, 1958).

35. See Peter N. Stearns' essay, 'Working Class Women in Britain 1890-1914,' in *Suffer and Be Still,* M. Vicinus (ed.) (Bloomington, 1972).

36. C.W. Cunnington, *Feminine Attitudes in the Nineteenth Century* (London, 1935), p. 10.

37. Doris Mary Stenton, *The English Woman in History* (London, 1957).

38. A good brief survey of the political struggle of women is in William O'Neill's *The Woman Movement: Feminism in the United States and England* (Chicago, 1969).

39. H. Perkin, *The Origins of Modern English Society 1780-1880* (London, 1969).

40. Patricia Thomson, *The Victorian Heroine, A Changing Ideal 1837-1873* (London, 1956).

41. Peter Laslett, *The World We Have Lost* (New York, 1960), p. 87.

42. *A New System of Practical Domestic Economy Founded on Modern Discoveries and the Private Communications of Persons of Experience* (London, 1828), p. vii.

43. Sarah Strickney Ellis, *The Women of England, Their Social Duties and Domestic Habits* (London, 1839).

44. *Ibid. passim.*

45. Isabella Beeton, *The Book of Household Management* (London, 1861).

46. Eliza Warren, *How I Managed My House on Two Hundred Pounds a Year* (London, 1864).

47. Eliza Warren, *How I Managed My Children From Infancy to Marriage* (London, 1865).

48. Alexis Soyer, *The Modern Housewife or Ménagère* (New York, 1849).

49. Sarah Strickney Ellis, *The Daughters of England* (London, 1845), *The Wives of England* (London, 1846), *The Mothers of England* (London, 1845).

50. John Walsh, *A Manual of Domestic Economy: Suited to Families Spending from £100 to £1000 a Year* (London, 1857); *A Manual of Domestic Economy: Suited to Families Spending From £150 to £1,500 a Year,* new ed. 1873, 1890.

51. Isabella Beeton, op. cit. (London, 1861, 1863, 1869, 1880, 1888, 1892, 1906, 1923, 1950).

52. Described in Janet Dunbar's *The Early Victorian Woman, Some Aspects of Her Life 1837-1857* (London, 1957), p. 72.

53. *The Englishwoman's Domestic Magazine* (April 1861), Preface (hereafter referred to as EDM).

54. *The Family Friend,* Volume VII (July-December 1858), Preface.

55. Harrison, op. cit.; Best, op. cit.; Crow, op. cit.

56. Warren, *Managed My House . . .*

57. Beeton, op. cit.

58. Roy Lewis, Edmund Upton and Angus Maude, *The English Middle Classes* (London, 1949).

59. Harrison, op. cit.; Best, op. cit.

60. Banks, op. cit., pp. 100-101.

61. Perkin, op. cit.

62. Harrison, op. cit., pp. 104-5.

63. R.S. Neale in his article 'Class and Class-Consciousness in Early Nineteenth Century England; Three Classes or Five?' in *Victorian Studies*, Vol. XII, No. 1 (September, 1968) finds the three-class structure inadequate in describing the middle class in the nineteenth century. David Lockwood's *The Black Coated Worker: A Study in Class Consciousness* (London, 1966), is a good study of one important segment of the lower middle-class clerks.

2 DO'S AND DON'TS FOR THE MISTRESS OF THE HOUSE

As mistress of the house, the middle-class woman gained a new position in society. Her personal influence grew greatly, as overnight she became an important decision-maker in her realm of home and family. Instead of obeying orders, the middle-class woman now gave directions to servants and tradesmen. For the first time in her life she was responsible for very important sums of money. Her power lay in her control over the household budget, but this could be a source of frustration as well. Direction of the household also included a number of demanding physical tasks and, usually, the employment of a servant. The middle-class housewife was thus an active agent in the family, not a pampered woman of leisure, yet her functions could easily outstrip her means.

The importance of the role of mistress of the house was widely acclaimed in nineteenth-century English society. The household manuals, which were really a product of the new functions of middle-class women, were naturally most explicit in their emphasis on the importance of her position.

Yet the household manuals produced a curious misconception about the middle-class housewife. They reflected real problems and responsibilities, as we shall see; above all they talked of the two greatest difficulties in household direction, budget management and the direction of servants. They gave a host of even more practical advice as well, by providing recipes and patterns. Hence, if for no other reason, they were widely read and elicited letters from ordinary women which reflected persistent concerns. Yet, beyond the recipe level, most of the advice in the manuals was irrelevant, aimed at a group above the real middle class. Above all, the tone of most manuals was naggingly critical of middle-class women. For if her household responsibilities were consistently recognized, her abilities to meet them were almost as regularly challenged. These various elements must all be sketched in this brief discussion of the manuals, for all may have had an impact on the middle-class readership.

There was a great deal of discussion in the nineteenth century on the middle-class housewife and her domestic problems, and the consensus among the critics was that the nineteenth-century middle-class woman had lost the treasured art of housekeeping. The Victorian woman was compared constantly to some woman of a past golden age who was her superior in every way; a healthier, happier, and a far more efficient housekeeper. The criticism of the middle-class housewife grew quite intense in the second half of the century. In the 1880s, a very popular and outspoken critic, in a series of articles which first appeared in *The*

Saturday Review and later in a two-volume work entitled *The Girl of the Period*, lamented that

> ... things are getting worse not better, and our young women are less useful than their mothers, while these last do not as a rule, come near the housekeeping ladies of older times, who knew every secret of domestic economy, and made a wise and pleasant distribution of bread their great point of honour.[1]

She sardonically went on to bemoan that

> ... it is strange to see into what unreasonable disrepute active housekeeping — women's first social duty — has fallen in England. The snobbish half of the middle-class hold housewifely work as degrading. A woman may sit in a dirty drawing room which the slip-shod maid has not had the time to clean, but she can not have a duster in her hands. There is no disgrace in the dust only in the duster.[2]

How did the middle-class woman in the nineteenth century come to lose the art of housekeeping? According to most of her critics, it was due to the lack of a proper education. The debate concerning the middle-class woman's education was wide and varied. Most of the authorities on domestic matters agreed that the middle-class girl's education was too 'ornamental.' The typical complaint was that

> ... too frequently in the middle classes we have instances of young women whose education has completely unfitted them for their sphere, by a process simply ornamental. They have been rendered indolent, useless and a disgrace to their connexions.[3]

An ornamental education was one that involved little more than music, singing, dancing, fancy needlework and some familiarity with a foreign language.

This criticism of the middle-class girl's education was part of a general criticism of the middle-class life style. Throughout the period the middle class, and in particular the middle-class woman, was criticized for its reckless extravagance, for living in a manner which was beyond its means and trying always to imitate the upper class. It was believed that the worries and disappointments that vexed the middle class were a result of their trying to appear 'better off' than they really were.[4] Education was one of the obvious ways in which the middle class aped the manners of the upper class. Middle-class parents desiring to improve their social standing would send their daughters off to boarding schools, to insure that they became 'ladies.' Many of the manuals warned parents that they must

> ... think seriously of what may be the real position of their children, not encourage ambitious hopes which are never

likely to be realized. The great aim in their rearing should
be to instill a fondness for home and domestic associations.[5]
A boarding school education did not afford the young girl the necessary
knowledge;

> . . . shut up in a school room with a French grammar and a
> piano as instruments of torture . . . the young girl loses the
> influence of household life and knows as little how to cook
> a dinner as to cure a cold. Both however, were part of every
> day life with which sooner or later they will probably have
> to cope.[6]

According to Mrs. Warren, a popular writer on domestic matters, the
proper education of a middle-class girl should teach her first how to
make and mend clothes, wash, bake, and cook, economically and well,
to clean and scour. This was the oil by which the domestic machinery
efficiently and noiselessly revolved each day,[7] and it was neglect of
this pragmatic education that set the basis for the later troubles of
middle-class women, according to many contemporary observers.

With this general hostility to the presumed middle-class life style
well established, the manuals sought to apply their comments to
actual household management. Here is where their interests and those
of their readers did to some extent converge. Readers solicited advice,
for example, about how to find a good servant. The following letter,
written to the *Housekeeper's Magazine*, described the problem:

> Sir — I have been for a long time desirous of procuring that
> great, useful, and extraordinary curiosity, a rough, plain
> laborious, old-fashioned servant maid; and having in vain
> looked out for a specimen of this genius, either in town or
> country, for twenty years, have at last come to the
> resolution of applying to *The Housekeeper's Magazine* and
> requesting, through the medium of its pages, such assistance
> as may enable me to obtain the subject of my search![8]

Other letters asked for recommendations on planning a budget. A
typical inquiry was a letter from 'Housekeeper' asking the readers of
the EDM for advice on how to make an allowance of £4.1s. per week
cover the expenses of four people.[9] From the manuals' standpoint,
questions of this sort were an ideal focus for the application of the
general criticisms of the housewife; budget discussions, particularly,
allowed frequent blasts against extravagance. Ironically, however, the
manuals usually mistook their audience. They talked about the upper
end of the middle class, which may indeed have seemed most
threatening to the established order in their ability to approach upper-
class spending patterns. But, as we will see, this left most of the middle
class unaided, except in so far as its members could benefit from
general recommendations on household accounts or the employment of

24

servants.

Neither of the two specific problems which, by mutual agreement of authors and readers, deserved most attention was new to the nineteenth century. Women had dealt both with servants and with household budgets in the past. However, the situation in the nineteenth century was indeed different from prior periods because now more women than ever before were in a position to assume these responsibilities. For the first time in any society, a very considerable portion of its members could turn their attention to the problem of disposing of surplus income as the middle class grew steadily and commanded increasing total wealth.[10] The specific point is not just that more people were making more money but that this brought about a new style of living which profoundly affected the middle class, as will be shown in this discussion.

The rise of domestic servants serves most dramatically to indicate the novelty of the middle-class situation. In the eighteenth century domestic service was largely restricted to the aristocracy. By 1850 the number of families that could afford domestic servants had greatly increased — hence, the rise in the number of domestic servants, which was much greater than the general population increase. In 1801 domestic servants totalled only 100,000; by 1851 the number was up to 1,300,000 and by 1881 it had reached 2,000,000.[11] The change in financial situation cannot be traced so vividly, given the lack of precise budget information on the middle class. But we will see that, in addition to seeking food, housing, and clothing above subsistence levels, the middle class tried to move into other categories of expenditure, particularly with regard to household appliances. Clearly, unfamiliarity with above-subsistence earnings, particularly when confronted with a growing variety of consumer goods, accounted for many of the difficulties middle-class families sensed. For many women, it was the first time that they had money to spend on provisions beyond the basic necessities or had come into contact with domestic servants. This is why they sought advice on these subjects. The advice they received is important in helping us to determine the intricacies of the problems and how the middle-class woman was expected to handle them.

The manuals heralded the Victorian woman's concern for keeping track of most family expenses by creating a new science, Domestic Economy. It was not a difficult science to learn, for it consisted simply of laying out to the greatest advantage the revenue which was appropriate to the domestic establishment, or so the manuals insisted. However, the practice of domestic economy was a bit more involved than this, especially for those on a limited income. Detailed planning and careful keeping of accounts became the norm for the middle class in running their households as in their businesses.

The key to household management, as stated in the manuals, was economy and frugality; 'Frugality and Economy are Home Virtues without which no household can prosper.'[12] The necessity of practising economy was considered vital to everyone, whether in the possession of an income no more than sufficient for a family's requirement, or a large fortune which put financial adversity out of the question. The philosophy was that it was never how much money one had but rather how one handled it which determined domestic happiness. Guidelines were set for the young mistress of the house to follow.

The first rule of domestic economy was to plan one's expenditures rationally. To do this properly it was recommended that the woman keep an account of all her daily expenditures, which should include every shilling and sixpence laid out. The keeping of the account book was guaranteed to take the mystery out of managing of finances.[13] The authorities on domestic economy generally believed that the reason women had such difficulty with their money affairs was that they did not properly organize them. A woman must be able to look at her financial situation as a whole and in detail, which is why such importance was placed upon the housekeeping account book.

Early in the century, the household manuals gave directions on how to make up one's account book. Columns for every article purchased for every day of the year were to be entered. By mid-century, ruled and printed books were being sold specifically for this purpose. The *Domestic Account Book* was typical, containing twenty-four divisions for such items as Bread and Flour, Butter and Cheese, Beer, Rent, Taxes, and Servants' wages.[14] A ledger was suggested also to record the various payments made to specific tradespeople, for example, Butcher, Baker, Milkman. This ledger afforded the mistress protection from dishonest tradesmen. If the woman had no account for each tradesman, it would be impossible to check them and an error made either wilfully or by mistake could neither be detected nor remedied.[15] It is difficult to determine how widely used these accounting books were but it should be noted that many of them were made and purchased as gift items. Here, then, is an area where the manuals' recommendations and the housewife's need for financial order often coincided.

Of course, accounting was useless without budgeting. This aspect of domestic economy gave it the appearance of being an exact science. Budgets were a predominant feature in many household manuals and they covered a wide range of incomes. One of the first manuals (1828) to systematize a series of budgets began with the income level of £55 and went up to £5000.[16] Two samples of budgets found in the 1828 manual and an 1874 manual are given in Table II. They show how a family of five in 1828 and a family of six in 1874 were advised to lay out their money.

TABLE II
Sample Budgets for Years 1828 – 1874

1828   £150 Per Year[17]

Items	Weekly		Annually		
	s	d	£	s	d
Bread, flour	5	0			
Milk, butter, cheese	4	4½			
Tea, coffee	2	0			
Sugar	2	4			
Grocery	1	8			
Butcher's meat & fish	7	7			
Vegetables, fruits	2	1			
Coals, wood	2	9			
Soap, starch	0	9			
Sundries	0	7			
Candles	0	9			
Clothes			24	0	0
Rent, taxes			15	0	0
Servant			3	0	0
Illness, amusement			3	14	0
Education & Private expenses			5	0	0
Reserve			12	0	0

1874   £150 Per Year[18]

Items	Annually		
	£	s	d
Bread	12	0	0
Milk, butter, cheese	10	0	0
Grocery	10	0	0
Greengrocery	8	0	0
Butcher's meat	30	0	0
Wine, spirits	1	0	0
Beer	8	0	0
Washing	3	0	0
Chandlery	3	0	0
Rent, taxes	17	10	0
Clothing	17	10	0
Servant's wages	10	0	0
Illness, amusement	10	0	0

The principle upon which the 1828 budget was based was to divide the whole income, whatever it was, into twelve equal parts; and of the expenditures per week, in every estimate, that of the parents was 8/12 and that for each child 1/12 or 3/12 in all. The remaining 1/12 was for reserve. The greater of 2/3 assigned to the parents not only included all the articles of provision for themselves, but also every other category of household expense, together with clothes, rent and all extras, while the 1/12 for each child consisted chiefly of provisions of the following kind — bread, flour, rice, oatmeal, sugar, treacle, milk, butter, potatoes, and all other vegetables.[19]

The 1874 principle of dividing up one's income was far more simple and the one most often cited: 1/2 of the annual income was reserved for the supplies of the house, 1/8 for rent and taxes, 1/8 for clothing, 1/8 for illness and amusement, 1/8 for wages, incidental expenses and charities.[20]

Even though the 1828 method of budgeting was more complicated, it did provide more useful information than the later method. In addition to dividing the income on a weekly basis, it listed how much bread, flour and butter was to be allotted for each person. This type of information was certainly of value for those on a narrow budget. The lack of these specifics in the later manuals might have limited their utility for the middle-class housewife, since letters appeared regularly asking for this type of information.[21]

Other advice from the manuals was of more dubious utility, for it could counter to the needs and aspirations of middle-class women. Prompt paying of bills was urged, for it was noted that irregularity in this matter often contributed to the financial destruction of the family.[22] The middle-class woman was advised that

> ... she is happy and blessed among women who 'pays as she goes' and never has one single thing she cannot pay for on the spot. Because bills shorten one's life and spoils one's temper.[23]

Detailed rules for marketing were recommended, and many of the prices quoted in the budgets were based on the ability to know how to make bulk purchases at the most appropriate time. For example, candles and soap should be purchased once a year, in the summer, when they were cheapest. And from this, of course, it was easy to belittle the ordinary shopper who did not know that the most economical method of shopping was to 'lay in stock for the week, in lieu of purchasing, as so many do, from hour to hour.'[24] How many middle-class women had the cash, not to mention the expertise, to buy in bulk is open to question.

The most likely distinction between the rather traditionalist pieties of the manuals and the actual habits of Victorian women concerned buying on time. The manuals, particularly during the first half of the century, urged cash purchases. The sentiment expressed was that 'it should be an invariable rule in domestic economy never to obtain anything on credit, for those who take credit generally pay an enormous interest for so doing.'[25] At the same time women's periodicals such as the EDM made frequent references to instalment buying, noting at one point, for example, that some stores were willing to give a discount as high as 15 per cent for those with ready money.[26] The extent of instalment buying during the ninteenth century has not yet been determined, but we do know that it was practised and that it spread rapidly during the second half of the century. And, as we will see, it must have made sense to a number of hard-pressed middle-class women.

These then were the general rules of domestic economy as found in the household manuals, which changed very little during the nineteenth century. If the middle-class woman followed these rules she would presumably have no problems with managing her finances, but the extent to which she did so is difficult to determine. They required that she be adept with mathematical skills and able to give the strictest attention to the most minute details, especially for those in the lower income levels, in order to maintain economic solvency. In this sense the manuals' advice was indeed useful, if difficult to follow. But whether middle-class woman had enough time and money to follow much of this advice, indeed whether they remained as wedded to traditional rules of domestic economy in some particulars, is open to question.

The one thing that is certain is that, in spite of all the sage advice, the middle-class woman's problems with finances not only persisted but grew in intensity as the period progressed. The number of middle-class families had increased steadily during the nineteenth century, so that more and more women were confronted for the first time with the problem of disposing of income; the problem, however, went deeper than this, and must be taken up again in the next chapter. For now, the main point is that the manuals' advice was not particularly helpful. They identified a problem. They gave advice on accounting procedures that could be useful. And they continued to preach against needless luxury and extravagance. But they rarely talked about what should be done with a small margin over necessity and, in their hostility to social climbing, they failed to guide women in the development of new material goals. These goals were developing, but far below the level of ostentation that preoccupied the manuals. Even an unusually sensitive comment, which did recognize some of the inevitable pressures on middle-class families and was relatively free of cant, failed to offer a remedy:

> Owing to the increasing wealth of the wealthy, and the
> increasing number who every year step into the wealthier
> class, the *style of living* as well as the cost of necessaries
> and comforts of which 'living' consists, has advanced in an
> extraordinary ratio; and however frugal, however, unostentatious,

however rational we may be, however resolute to live as we
think we ought, and not as others do around us, it is, as we
shall find, simply impossible not to be influenced by their
example and to fall into their ways, unless we are content
either to live in remote districts or in an isolated fashion. The
result is that we need many things that our fathers did not,
and that for each of these many things we must pay more.
Even where prices are lower, quantities are increased.[27]

And so 'life at high pressure' went on, with most advice offered to
women only creating a sense of guilt that the budget was not under
better control.

Problems with domestic servants were as endemic as difficulties with
household finance, and again the manuals recognized this fact. The
pervasiveness of these problems received amusing comment in an 1835
article in the *Magazine of Domestic Economy*, which observed that

What topic — always excepting our national subject, 'the
weather', is so unfailing in conversation, as that of servants,
and their faults? Every country town is 'the worst place in
the world for servants', while in London, we hear, 'they
become more and more insolent and worthless every day. . .[28]

The complaints grew louder as the century progressed. In the 1850s an
essay lamented that

. . . the cry is common, and too true that there are 'few
good servants to be had now-a-days', and the question
naturally follows 'Why is it so?' 'Is it the fault of
employers or of servants?'[29] What is wrong? and what is
the cause of the wrong? The 'Great Servant Question', as it
is called, has been brought forward, opinions have been given,
and suggestions made, and with what result?[30]

In 1899 there was even a session at the Industrial Section of the
International Congress of Women on the 'Scientific Treatment of
Domestic Service.' The problem was stated to be twofold: 1. There
were not enough servants; 2. The servants that were available were not
good enough.[31]

What was the cause of this persistent concern? Again the consensus
was that the fault lay with the mistress of the house. Some of the
typical comments were that 'this growing incompetence of servants
so loudly and so widely deplored, is very largely the result of the
growing incompetence of mistresses.'[32] 'It is the carelessness of the
mistress, which in nine cases out of ten makes the sin of the servant.'[33]
Eliza Warren, in her popular best seller, *How I Managed My House on
£200 per Year,* was of the same opinion. She remarked that

It is said that the race of good servants has died out, leaving
no successors. And why is this? It may be asked. Because

their teachers have died with them. Untaught young
mistresses are incapable of teaching.[34]

The mistress was guilty of many faults. She did not know how to
manage her home and therefore she did not know how to tell others to
do it for her. She was thoughtless and inconsiderate, often expecting
far too much from her servant. She was the major cause of 'the greatest
plague in life.'[35] However, in spite of the consistency of the complaints,
most of the manuals claimed that the problem was not inevitable. If
the mistress would abandon her apathy and idle moaning and follow the
advice of the manuals, a good relationship was possible and indeed vital
to the running of a proper home. The manuals did, to be sure, offer
constructive suggestions, but often of the most general nature. They
urged that the mistress be careful in her selection of servants, choosing a
person with 'integrity, sobriety, cleanliness, and general propriety in
manner and dress and a knowledge of the duties of the prospective
department of household management.'[36] How was such a paragon to
be found? Most manuals recommended that the employer inquire
among her friends or local tradesmen, though one series of articles noted
that some tradesmen gave references for servants who had incurred the
disfavor of their previous employers, in return for a fee or the promise
that the servant would bring in the household's trade.[37] Registry offices
for placement were not considered respectable by the manuals, though
they did exist.

This meant, as the manuals recognized, that most mistresses had
only one means of determining the suitability of a prospective servant,
which was through her 'character,' a form of reference from her previous
mistress. Hence, as one manual stated, the mistress was warned 'to be
minute in her investigation of the character she received and equally
cautious and scrupulously just in giving one to another.'[38] But
characters themselves were unreliable. Many former employers were
reluctant to cause trouble for their servants, and some may have feared
legal problems if they gave a bad character. Hence, by the second half
of the century, it became the general opinion that 'characters are
perfectly worthless.' Mrs. Beeton suggested that written characters be
supplemented by an interview with the former mistress, which would
help in the assessment of the servant and also in judging the quality of
this person's household, as a means of testing her own basis for judge-
ment. 'Negligence and want of cleanliness in her and her household
generally will naturally lead you to the conclusion, that her servant has
suffered from the influence of the bad example.'[39] But in truth, there
was no good remedy.

Beyond the difficult attempt to hire a good servant in the first place,
the manuals recommended that the servants' duties be spelled out
carefully in advance. For example, Mrs. Beeton advised that

> We would here point out an error — and a grave one it is —
> into which some mistresses fall. They do not, when engaging
> a servant, expressly tell her all the duties to which she will
> be expected to perform. This is an act of omission severely
> to be reprehended. Every portion of work which the maid
> will have to do should be plainly stated by the mistress and
> understood by the servant.[40]

Many of the manuals accordingly went into great detail, describing the
various functions of the different types of servants in the domestic
hierarchy. Mrs. Beeton gave in-depth descriptions of the functions of the
following domestics: butler, footman, coachman, groom, stable boy,
valet, lady's maid, upper and under housemaid, maid-of-all-work, dairy-
maid, laundry-maid, upper and under nursemaid, sick nurse, wet nurse
and monthly nurse.

Finally, during the second half of the nineteenth century a number
of manuals dealt with increasing legal complexities in the employment
of servants, stressing the need for proper notice in termination of
employment and the grounds for legal dismissal.[41]

These categories of advice were not entirely irrelevant. The elaborate
discussions of servant's references reflected a real problem, and given
the labor market actual mistresses had no better luck resolving it than
did the manuals. But the desirability of listing duties was obscured, for
most middle-class readers, by the fact that they simply did not employ
the kinds of specialized servants that the manuals went to such trouble
to describe. Legal problems were closer to the mark again, but they
reflected difficulties most likely to occur in a complex household and,
probably, with male servants. The laments of middle-class women,
which did reflect their unfamiliarity with their situation as employers,
were much more prosaic. In one letter a housewife inquired

> I shall be much obliged by early answers to the following
> questions: If I give a servant a month's notice, and send her away
> before the end of that month, must I pay her board wages until
> the end of her time? If so, how much? Also, can a servant demand
> cab fare and railway fare back to the place she comes from?[42]

Another young housekeeper wanted information on the proper
allowances for servants, asking:

> Is it customary for servants always to have egg, fish, or ham, etc.
> for their breakfast? Also a pudding to their dinner? Would it not
> be better to make them a *plainer* pudding? Also, when the
> washing is done at home, is it usual   for domestics to get as
> much starch as they please for their own gowns and petticoats?
> Is it correct that servants always have the evenings to themselves?
> About holidays — which are they *really* entitled to? And
> what about allowances — is 1 lb. of sugar and 3/4 lb. of butter

the right amount for each servant weekly?[43]
To concerns of this sort the manuals paid relatively little attention,
although they did give suggested wage lists from time to time.

Most important, again, is the fact that, on the all-important question
of the quality of servants' work, the manuals turned primarily to the
treatment the mistress meted out. Here was the real problem, and the
criticism was typically intense. The famous Mrs. Ellis was especially
severe in her criticism of the middle-class mistress's treatment of
servants. She remarked that

> Servants are generally looked upon, by thoughtless young
> ladies, as a sort of household machinery, and when that
> machinery is of sufficient extent to operate upon every
> branch of the establishment there can be no reason why
> it should not be brought into exercise, and kept in motion
> to any extent that may not be injurious. This machinery,
> however, is composed of an individual possessing heart as
> susceptible of certain kinds of feelings, as those of the more
> privilege being to whose comfort and convenience it is their
> daily business to minister.[44]

The typical lament of the critics was that the old paternalistic relationship
between mistress and maid was dying and being replaced by a cold
business arrangement. Too many mistresses believed that their only
responsibility to their servant was to pay them their wages. Mistresses
never took the time to acquaint themselves with the worries or joys of
their servants. They no longer extended over them the same watchful
protection and the same kind of solitude as in prior times.[45] When were
mistresses going to remember that 'Good servants are to be sought not
only by money but by money's worth . . .'[46] In other words, the
manuals applied to their discussion of servants the same sense of
deterioration, given the rise of a new middle class, that they developed
in more general arguments. New women, not born to their place, could
not direct servants in proper fashion. Some of these criticisms may have
been appropriate, for inexperienced mistresses could easily have
neglected or even mistreated their charges. But there is little independent
evidence that this was so, at least in comparison with the eighteenth
century, on any general level. The laments for a lost paternalism are
particularly suspect. Above all, since we cannot here be concerned with
a thorough assessment of the servants' lot, the manuals' approach had
little utility for the middle-class woman and may have done little even
to correct abusive treatment. For the manuals failed to deal with the
real middle-class situation. They did not discuss in any detail the kinds
of servants middle-class women employed, and they therefore virtually
ignored the vast change in the servant labor force during the ninteenth
century.

After 1850, objections to the common approach found their way into print, holding that the servant problem was not entirely the fault of the mistress. A few essays went so far as to claim that it was the mistress who was disadvantaged, because the modern servant came from the dregs of the lower classes, even from the ranks of outright criminals.[47] An important article, entitled 'Our Servants,' reflected the attitudes of those mistresses who had tried all the standard recommendations:

> I now offer the result of my experience as a 'mistress of a household', and as having devoted time, energy, and health to the task of improving servants, while there has been no result but ingratitude on their side, and disappointment on mine. I simply say to those of my readers who would do the same, 'Don't try it. Be just to your servants, and expect obedience from them, but anything that you may do for them beyond their 'rights' any concession you make to them is simply thrown away. Perhaps it does positive harm by weakening your authority and lessening the distance between you.' Friends in servants, indeed! Expect servants to be our friends! I have tried, but it cannot be; it is not in their nature to soften or yield to kindness.[48]

The disappointed mistress went on to say she was sick and tired of the nonsense about the poor condition of domestic service, that servants were treated as slaves by mistresses who were no better than tyrants. The truth was that servants were better off than any other sector of the working community, and at the same time the most insolent and unappreciative.

The frustrations of the mistress with her domestic servant was also a theme developed by Eliza Warren in several of her works. In her book *Comfort for Small Incomes* she related similar experiences with the same fruitless results as that of the outspoken mistress above. Mrs. Warren was forced to make the same conclusions and warned mistresses that 'good servants suitable for middle-class families were not to be had . . .'[49]

Here is the problem writ large for us. What was the true situation facing the middle-class housewife? Were incompetence and reckless extravagance the real causes behind her continuing financial woes? Was her thoughtlessness the source of her servant problem? It is obvious that much of the criticism found in the manuals and domestic magazines echoes our image of the Victorian woman, with the important qualification that the manuals recognized that the woman was charged with a variety of important functions. The manuals found the woman wanting in her functions because of poor training and ostentation; this is not perhaps too far from the conventional historical view that Victorian women had few functions of any sort. If we could move only from uselessness to failure we would not, perhaps, advance historical understanding significantly. But, as we have already suggested, the manuals were often misleading. They raise some of the real problems middle-class women faced, but their general tone was persistently colored by the conviction that women were going astray in the modern world. This in itself is interesting. It reflects change, even if the change was misinterpreted; it reflects the fact that the middle-class housewife was gradually trying to forge a new style of life. Why the manuals adopted such a critical stance toward change is not easy to answer, and suggests a need to look at the background of the authors, including their relationship to older groups such as the clergy which offered moral advice. The impact of the hostile tone on middle-class readers is another ambiguous problem to which we shall return. Certainly the barrage of criticism could have been unnerving to women eager for advice on activities new to them.

Above all, we cannot stop with the manual literature because it was too often focused on an upper-class, rather than middle-class situations. Here is doubtless one reason for the frequent criticisms, for the manuals often used as examples types of people who were open to social climbing. Middle-class women, if they climbed, aspired to no such heights. Even some contemporaries noted this disparity.

We turn, then, to an attempt to go beneath the standard rhetoric and to grasp the actual situation of the middle-class woman herself.

Notes

1. E. Lynn Linton, *The Girl of the Period and Other Social Essays*, Vol. I & II (London, 1883), pp. 38-9.
2. Ibid., p. 43.
3. *Economy for the Single and Married,* p.99
4. *Health and Home* [by a Quiet Woman] (London, 1875), p. 104.
5. *Economy for the Single and Married*, p. 44.
6. *The Hand-Book of Women's Work* [ed. by L.M.H.] (London, 1876), pp. 6-7.
7. Warren, *Managed My House*, Preface.
8. *The Housekeeper's Magazine and Family Economist*, (London, 1826), p. 60.
9. *The Englishwoman's Domestic Magazine*, (October 1871).
10. Checkland, *The Rise of Industrial Society*, p. 314.
11. Perkin, *The Origins of English Society*, p. 143.
12. Beeton, *Household Management*, p. 2.
13. *Economy for the Single and Married*, pp. 35-6.
14. *Domestic Account Book* was printed in 1843 and sold for 2s.
15. Walsh, *Manual of Domestic Economy* (1874), p. 692.
16. *A New System of Practical Domestic Economy* (London, 1828).
17. *A New System of Domestic Economy*, p. 424.
18. Walsh, *Manual of Domestic Economy*, (1874), p. 677.
19. *A New System of Practical Domestic Economy*, pp. 393-4.
20. Walsh, *Manual of Domestic Economy*, (1874), p. 676.
21. One such letter appeared in the *British Mothers' Journal* (February, 1858) asking how much bread and meat *per diem* was to be allotted to a family of four, p. 56.
22. John Armstrong, *The Young Woman's Guide to Virtue, Economy and Happiness*, (Newcastle Upon Tyne, 1817), p. 46.
23. Jane Ellen Frith Panton, *Leaves From a Housekeeper's Book*, (London, 1914), p. 102.
24. *Economy for the Single and Married*, p. 40.
25. *The Housekeeper's Magazine*, p. 2.
26. *Englishwoman's Domestic Magazine*, Vol. 7 (1869), p. 101.
27. W.R. Gregg, 'Life at High Pressure,' in *The Contemporary Review*, (March, 1875), p. 633.
28. *The Magazine of Domestic Economy* (1835-36), p. 211.
29. *British Mothers' Journal*, (May, 1859), p. 105.
30. *The Mother's Companion*, (London, 1890), p. 132.
31. Emily James (ed.), *Englishwoman's Year Book and Directory 1899-1900* (London, 1900), p. 91.
32. *Health and Home*, p. 170.
33. *Home Difficulties: or Whose Fault is it? A few Words on the Servant Question* [by the Author of 'A Woman's Secret'] (London 1866), p. 8.
34. Warren, *Managed My House*, Preface.
35. Beeton, *Household Management*, p. 961.
36. T. Webster, *An Encyclopaedia of Domestic Economy, Comprising Such Subjects as are Most Immediately Connected with Housekeeping* (New York, 1845), p. 347.
37. *Domestic Servants, As They Are and As They Ought To Be* (By a practical mistress of a household) (Brighton, 1859), p. 15.
38. Armstrong, *Young Woman's Guide*, p. 47.
39. Beeton, *Household Management*, p. 7. Other manuals which offered the same advice were *Ward & Lock's Home Book* (London, 1880), p. 347; Warren

Managed My House, p. 54.

40. Beeton, *Household Management*, p. 7. The recommendation was also stressed in *Ward & Lock's Home Book*, p. 317

41. Walsh's *Manual of Domestic Economy*, had a detailed section on the laws concerning servants and masters, pp. 227-8, as did *Ward & Lock's Home Book*, section 529, entitled 'The Law of Masters and Servants,' p. 348.

42. *Englishwoman's Domestic Magazine*, (April 1869), p. 222.

43. Ibid. (December 1871), p. 381.

44. Ellis, *Women of England*, p. 15.

45. *The British Mother's Journal of 1859*, (October 1859), p. 232.

46. *Englishwoman's Domestic Magazine*, Vol. VII (May-October 1863), p. 158.

47. *British Mother's Journal*, (May 1859), p. 105.

48. *The British Mothers' Family Magazine for 1864*, p. 270.

49. Eliza Warren, *Comfort for Small Incomes*, (London, 1866), p. 14.

3 THE MODERN HOMEMAKER

The role of the married middle-class woman as mistress of the house can be evaluated only on the basis of a clear understanding of the material culture of the class. For a key flaw in contemporary and subsequent impressions about the middle-class lies in the complete neglect of the actual economic definition of the middle-class in the nineteenth century. This does not mean that values are to be ignored; they will continue to form a substantial part of this study. But the middle-class has been defined too long in terms of values alone.[1] This study, in attempting to understand the situation of the middle-class, needs to determine how the Victorian woman actually lived, not how we think she should have lived, nor, for the moment, how she thought she should live. If we do not understand her material base we cannot know if the values so often discussed applied to the whole group.

Invocation of the term middle-class raises possible problems for any general study, even in terms of material conditions and certainly in the areas of broader values. The middle-class was composed of distinct occupational subgroups. It was somewhat relatedly divided between old and new elements. Thus most clergymen, although broadly fitting material definitions of the middle-class, have to be marked off because of their professional status and their tendency to defend older canons of behavior; engineers, a newer group fighting for professional recognition, might well behave and think differently. These distinctions have been only tentatively explored for the middle-class in general, and only in one case, that of birth control, applied to women in particular.[2] In commenting on general material levels, as in our earlier discussion of the kind of advice directed at the middle-class woman, we do assume some shared attributes across occupational and new/old lines. But we will in later case studies be able to isolate some distinctions of behavior within the common range, and it has already been suggested that it was the older middle-class who produced much of the literature that has been held characteristic of the outlook of the class as a whole. If we are not yet in a position to measure internal divisions precisely, they should not be forgotten, even as we turn to the legitimate effort to isolate what middle-class women more generally encountered during this period of transition.

A more pervasive tendency in recent social and urban history leads more readily to a different, though not necessarily more important, objection to the present level of generalization. The host of studies of individual localities reveals, not surprisingly, that many different city types existed as England industrialized. Unfortunately, few reveal much about the middle-class specifically and almost none discusses women. An excellent recent comparative study of three localities focuses, predictably, on the working class alone.[3] More general urban studies allow us to contrast a growing borough such as Hampstead with the more stable country town of York, in terms of overall growth, building patterns and the like, but if they offer data on the behavior of groups of people (which urban historians often disdain) they rarely isolate individual classes.[4] A specific case study will be offered in this book, that of Camberwell, where we can illustrate some general claims about the health and childbirth patterns of middle-class women. But while readily admitting that further case studies would be desirable, applying the techniques of local history to subjects such as specific classes and sexes, there is no need to view the results of local histories so far as potentially destructive of the present effort at generalization. We do not need to wait for a brick-by-brick approach to indicate what the whole building looked like. Membership of the middle-class exposed women to a host of common experiences in the city. Hence, as already indicated, the common quest for advice on how to handle new problems and the production of national, not regional, literature for the class. Furthermore, some apparent local differences will on further analysis prove to be more susceptible to explanation by distinctions in class level than to the overweening influence of a particular town environment. Hampstead's population undeniably behaved differently from that of York, even if we follow the few comparative hints available about the middle-class specifically. But this results in the first instance from the fact that Hampstead had little middle-class at all, but rather an upper middle-class, despite the tendency to alternate the terms in the Hampstead study itself. The kinds of houses built, the numbers of servants employed indicate this quite clearly. None of this should discourage precise local studies. But a nominalist quest for the individual unit must not distract from the general characteristics of the English middle-class. And here we return to a material culture that was widely shared. The first problem to contend with in defining the middle class involves key income ranges within the class, ranges so great that the increasingly pressed groups at both the upper and lower extremities into distinct social categories. These ranges themselves, if firmly understood, can inform any further effort to use case studies to indicate the impact of locality or occupation on the more general trends of class behavior.

Admittedly, due to insufficient data on incomes for the nineteenth century, neat statistics on the average middle-class income cannot frame the discussion at the outset. What the nineteenth century considered middle-class has added greatly to the problem of definition. The range of opinions during the period was wide. A woman inquiring what was the lowest sum a 'lady and gentleman' could live on, was told by the respected EDM that by strict economy two persons could live on £200 per year, and others pretty comfortably on £400 and £500. It depended very much on the taste of the lady and gentleman. But it was certain that no one could live on less than the first mentioned sum.[5] According to another popular contemporary source £500 a year was a 'modest' income.[6] Mrs. Belloc, in her work *Essays on Woman's Work*, noted that £100–£200 a year avoided absolute penury and described 'genteel merchants and second-rate professional men' as scraping by on £300–£400 a year.[7] The range of incomes found in the household manuals certainly adds to the confusion. As noted in the previous section, the manual *A New System of Practical Domestic Economy* listed eighteen different income levels, from £55–£5000 per year. What was middle-class?

Recent studies have quoted £300 per annum as the typical and minimal middle-class income.[8] However, this study contends that £300 was neither typical nor minimal, but rather the maximum income level of most middle-class families in the nineteenth century. The £300 income level grouped only a very small portion of the middle class and was really more representative of the upper middle class than the bulk of the class. In other words, at £300 people were close to what constituted at least a separate subgroup. They had distinctive opportunities – in education for example – that moved them close to the periphery of the upper class. And apart from such opportunities, the number of people attaining this level was simply too small to include what we properly regard as middle-class in terms of occupations and key values. Hence, it was necessary to expand the figure to include £100–£300 per year as more descriptive of the middle-class income range in nineteenth-century England. Since this is a crucial point to the whole study, the limited nature of the evidence is obviously unfortunate. But due to the many problems one encounters with dealing with nineteenth-century statistical data, it is doubtful whether anything more precise can ever be established, save perhaps in local studies using personal records.

It would be logical to turn to the two most obvious sources of statistical data for the period, census returns and tax records. But the problems of using this material for social stratification are almost overwhelming. For example, census material is often unreliable because the methods of taking the census and the classification of the population frequently changed in the nineteenth century, thereby making it difficult to draw comparisons. A greater problem with the census material for this particular study was its lack of class-specific data. Generally, there was no clear division of classes at all; for instance, under the industrial sector, which is of prime importance for the nineteenth century due to its tremendous growth rate, manufacturers and workers were listed together. For their part, the statistical accuracy of tax returns is thoroughly questionable. There were numerous loopholes in the tax structure which allowed many people to pay little or no taxes. In addition to the problem of tax evasion, the adequacy of the tax returns in determining the incomes received by income tax payers is impaired by the idiosyncracies of their compilation. A single individual, for instance, might easily be assessed under more than one schedule, as an owner of property perhaps in Schedule A and as a recipient of an earned income in Schedule D, and thus appear in the tax returns as two persons.[9]

There were two independent studies made in the nineteenth century which attempted to analyse classes and incomes. Even though they cannot pretend to the statistical accuracy of a modern social survey they offer a beginning to a better interpretation of what was middle-class in the nineteenth century. The earliest study on incomes in the nineteenth century was for the year 1803 made by Patrick Colquhoun, entitled *A Treatise on Indigence.*[10] It is an extremely valuable source because it offers the only information we have on the various occupations defined not only by class but also by annual income. The occupational breakdown alone is of great significance since the census returns for the first half of the century were very general and broad, listing all occupations under either agriculture, or trade and manufacturing, or others. According to Colquhoun's findings, which are listed in Table III, the majority of the middle-class in 1803 made less than £300 per year.

In looking over Colquhoun's data, it is obvious that he has included the agricultural community and tailors as part of his middle class. Strictly speaking, these were not part of the middle class in the nineteenth century. The relationship of prosperous farmers and the urban middle class deserves attention, for there may have been shared values and one could easily serve as a source for the other, as urbanization increased. Artisan masters, owning their own shops, might also relate to the lower levels of the middle class in more than income terms. But given the absence of precise work on the English middle-class to date, it is safest to be conservative and focus on the urban group that did not work with their hands.[11] The 320,000 families of the agriculture community and the 25,000 families representing tailors must be eliminated. This reduces the size of the middle-class substantially from Colquhoun's original figure of 634,640 families to 289,640 families. Even with this revision, the major point remains that the bulk of the middle-class in 1803 made less than £300 per year. Of the 289,640 middle-class families, 197,300 families, more than two-thirds (68 per cent of the total,) made between £100—£300 per year. The number of families making over £300 amounted to 60,340, which was only about one-fifth

(20.8 per cent) of the middle-class population in 1803. Thus one can begin to see why it is essential to expand the middle-class income range to include those families who made between £100 and £300 per year.

TABLE III
Colquhoun's Income and Occupation — 1803

Occupation	Income per Family Over 300	No. of Families
Merchants (1)	2600	2,000
Merchants (2)	800	13,000
Manufacturers	800	25,000
Warehousemen	800	500
Shipbuilders	500	5,000
Civil Offices	800	2,000
Law	350	11,000
Clergy	500	1,000
Education	600	500
Lunatic Keepers	500	40
		60,340
	100-300	
Agricultural Freeholder	200	40,000
Farmers	120	160,000
Surveyors, Engineers	200	5,000
Tailors	150	25,000
Shopkeepers	150	74,500
Inn-Keepers	100	50,000
Civil Offices	200	10,500
Clergy	120	12,500
Arts, Science	260	16,300
Education	150	20,000
Naval Office	149	3,000
Army Office	139	5,000
Theatrical	200	500
		422,300
	Under 100	
Agricultural Freeholder	90	120,000
Clerks	75	30,000
Half-pay Office	45	2,000
		634,640

Source: As reported by Harold Perkin in his work *The Origins of English Society*, pp. 20-21.

A comparison of Colquhoun's findings with a later study made by R.D. Baxter in 1868[12] indicates further the importance of the £100–£300 income level over the £300 plus income level in defining what was middle-class in the nineteenth century. There were many difficulties in working with the Baxter study.[13] Its accuracy is certainly questionable, since the author relied heavily upon tax returns for his information. However, until there is more original research into these records, we have to be content with Baxter's findings.[14] Baxter reported his findings for England in 1867 as follows:

Middle-Class Income Distribution 1867

No. of Families	Income Per Year
150,000	Over £300
850,500	£100–£300
1,003,000	Under £100
2,003,500	

Source: Baxter, *National Income*, p. 36. The number of families was based on the number of tax-payers — one tax-payer per family.

Before comparing Baxter to Colquhoun, it is necessary first to define Baxter's middle-class. He stated that his general rule for the classification of the population into the middle-class was to include the following: Officers, Agents, Learned Professions, Merchantile Men, Dealers, Tradesmen and persons who buy and sell, Masters, Superintendants, Collectors, Foremen, Clerks, Shopmen and Measurers.[15] Baxter enumerated the middle-class occupational groups, based on the 1861 census returns illustrated in Table IV. This table shows that some segments of Baxter's middle-class must be eliminated, as was done with Colquhoun's. Group II, Domestics, and Group IV, Agriculture were not part of the urban middle-class. However, as noted earlier the difficulty of eliminating the two groups was greater because Baxter never correlated his income figures with occupations. Since the agricultural segment and the domestic segment amounted to about one-fourth of the middle-class, as defined by Baxter, the two lower levels of income were reduced by one-fourth in order to compensate for these groups. In other words, in terms of the present argument about the importance of the lower income categories, the revision was effected in the most conservative way possible.

A comparison of the revised findings of Baxter and Colquhoun demonstrate dramatic changes in the middle class, as shown in the table below.

TABLE IV

Baxter's Middle Class According to Occupation

I.	Professional	Males Over 20 Years
1.	Government	50,497
2.	Army and Navy	13,340
3.	Learned Professions	146,815
II.	Domestics	
4.	Board and Lodging	72,627
III.	Commercial	
5.	Persons who buy and sell	130,820
6.	Conveyance	23,590
IV.	Agriculture	
7.	Land	218,431
8.	Animals	16,337
V.	Industrial	
9.	Art & Mechanical Products	76,471
10.	Textile and Dress	71,100
11.	Food and Drinks	176,308
12.	Animal Substance	400
13.	Vegetable Substance	14,161
14.	Mineral	56,297
VI.	Indefinite	
15.	Miscellaneous	4,459
16.	Foremen, Overlookers, Time Keepers	100,000

Source: Baxter, *National Income*, Appendix I, p. 82.

TABLE V

Middle-Class Income Distribution for Years 1803 and 1867

Income Per Year	#of Families — 1803	#of Families — 1867
Over £300	64,840	150,000
£100 — £300	197,300	637,875
Under £100	32,000	757,250
	294,140	1,540,125

It is apparent from the above table that the most significant change in terms of numbers was among the lower middle class, those who made under £100 per year. But, again to be cautious in extending our inquiry beyond the conventional view of the middle class, it was not judged safe to include this group in the direct analysis. There is too little known about its occupational situation or its age structure — for some were undoubtedly genuinely middle-class households just starting out and ideally some sense of evolution over time would enhance our understanding of middle-class women. But not all of these households were simply temporarily poor, and we know far too little, for this period, about what divided them from the working class, for in terms of income there was considerable overlap. For example, the highly skilled in the working class, defined by Baxter, made between £50 and £73 per year.[16] Thus, the middle class for this study was defined as making between £100 and £300 per year because this income level was clearly above the working-class wage and it embraced a sizable proportion of the middle class, in 1867 about 42 per cent. This is especially important in view of the fact that those conventionally defined as middle-class, families with an income over £300 per year, represented a small minority and had expanded less rapidly between 1803 and 1867 than the central segment. For the number of middle-class families in the £100–£300 range had increased significantly between 1803 and 1867. One example of the change can be seen in the growth of the professional ranks which rose from 74,000 families in 1803 to 210,682 in 1867, a rate of increase of 185 per cent.[17]

With this new economic definition of the middle class we can begin to put into perspective the criticism of the middle-class life style which has been repeated down to present time. One of the most obvious examples from the manuals, which has persisted in the conventional historical view of the Victorian middle-class woman's life, concerns her education. We have readily accepted, as most of the authorities on domestic management implied, that middle-class girls were sent off to boarding schools, where their minds were dulled by frivolous pastimes. But this was not true for the majority of middle-class girls. The middle class girl was educated in the home, usually by her mother.

There is a real need for an analytical study of the education of the middle-class girl in the nineteenth century. The studies to date have tended only to emphasize the reform movements in education,[18] which were not significant until very late in the century. We have also relied too often upon the fiction of the day for our information about education, as in other matters. In this instance, Becky Sharp's schooling is often cited as being typical of the education of middle-class girls. However, available references to actual boarding school costs reveal that they were almost uniformly well beyond the economic means of the majority of middle-class families. Frances Power Cobbe, for example, in her autobiography, quoted her bill for two years at a fashionable boarding school in Brighton in 1835 as £1000. The average price of a boarding school education has been cited as £130 per annum.[19] There were less expensive schools available, such as St. Margaret's College which advertised its ability to remedy the great deficiency in religious training and the neglect in the more solid parts of English education met within the Young Ladies Boarding schools. The financial arrangements were £60 per annum for girls under twelve and £70 per annum for those above twelve. There was an additional entrance fee of £3. These fees included medical attendance and every other expense except books and stationery.[20] Apparently there were schools who advertised costs as low as £25 to £30, according to a letter to the EDM which seriously questioned the quality of education at such places.[21] It can be seen from this designation of costs alone that we cannot generalize about boarding school education in the nineteenth century, for the differences were great. More important for our purposes, even the least expensive schools were well beyond the financial means of the bulk of middle-class families in the nineteenth century. Not many families could afford £25 a year to send their daughter off to school: for this would require a yearly expenditure of 8-25 per cent of the annual income for those families in the central segment of the middle class.[22]

Another type of education defined as typically middle-class was the home education by a governess. The novel *Aurora Leigh* is often cited as describing best this system for the middle-class girl.[23] The long discussions on how to choose the proper governesses in the many sources on domestic management certainly implied that this type of education was common among the middle class; and it has been suggested as a pattern in more recent studies.[24] However, it does not seem likely that this type of education was at all typical. First of all, there simply were not enough governesses to serve the bulk of the middle class, for according to the 1871 census there were only about 55,000 governesses in all.[25] Second, the cost of a governess made this tutorial system quite restrictive. The wage of a governess ranged from between £15—£100 per year, with the average wage centered in £20—£45 per year.[26] This again would require expenditures of from 8-25 per cent of the annual income, which was not economically feasible for any but the upper middle class.

Thus the manuals' criticism of the middle-class girl's education as being too ornamental certainly did not apply to those who made less than £300 per year. Their emphasis was clearly on the upper-class situation. Here is the first example of the failure to recognize the limited conditions that faced most middle-class girls. The criticism that middle-class women lost the art of housekeeping through their education is not just. As girls they spent much of their time in the home and were constantly exposed to household influence. No doubt there were some middle-class girls who were fortunate enough to live near a day school and could receive some type of formal education. But never for any length of time, a year at most. Generally, these schools were few and far between and thus could only service a small part of the middle class. The girl in the new large cities had to wait until a national system of education was established in the 1870s.[27]

The opportunity to acquire domestic skills was more available to the middle-class girl than any other accomplishment. If we are to understand the middle-class housewife of the nineteenth century, we must escape the generalized criticisms, for this woman could probably sew and cook and clean quite adequately. After all she spent most of her time doing household chores. All her days and many evenings were spent in scrubbing, dusting, tending to fires, for six to ten rooms in a three-to four-storey home, plus doing the cooking, shopping, washing, and sewing required for a family of five. It is true that many middle-class housewives had some help with their work but this assistance was not enough, as will be seen shortly. The work load in the middle-class home demanded full participation from the housewife and a diverse set of skills.

As the manuals did suggest, one of the most pressing responsibilities facing the mistress of the house in the nineteenth century was the managing of finances. There is no doubt that the manuals were correct in noting that the gravest problem, which destroyed many marriages, was economics. However, their interpretation of the financial problem was not relevant for the majority of middle-class families. The manuals judged the financial problem in terms of arrangement of money matters rather than insufficient funds, which was the real difficulty facing the middle-class housewife. The manuals did not spend enough time on the special problems of the lower levels of income, and so, ironically, the woman who most needed the information was sadly neglected.

A common economic problem facing the middle-class woman, who was for the first time the prime consumer in the new industrial urban community, was maintaining her position as the standard of living climbed. Generally the manuals failed to realize the problems involved in meeting the rising standard of living for those on a limited income. There was only one manual, *The Manual of Domestic Economy*,[28] which recognized that the standard of living had indeed risen. In 1873, in the second edition of the manual, the author stated that in order to meet the increased cost of living it was necessary to increase the original income levels of the 1854 edition of £100–£1000 to £150–£1500. His solution to the problem was theoretically satisfactory but hard to implement, for few middle-class families would be able to increase their

47

income by 50 per cent. The crux of the matter was that it was becoming more and more difficult to live on £150 in the second half of the century than it had been in the first half; for, because of improvements in the standard of living, the cost of maintaining a middle-class household had risen by as much as 50 per cent in the twenty years from 1850 to 1870 alone.[29] The woman's financial problems in the second half of the century included expenditures and increased expenses not even imagined in the first half of the century.

In order to understand fully the financial pressures facing the middle-class woman as manager of the family finances, it is necessary briefly to describe her increased expenses and the new purchases that became part of the middle-class life style, in the second half of the century. Our image of the middle-class life style has overemphasized the role of luxuries, especially those defined as the 'paraphernalia of gentility', thereby misrepresenting completely the nature of the financial problem facing the middle-class housewife. If one considers the budgets presented in the previous chapter, it can be seen immediately that there was very little money, if any, left over for luxury items. For example, in the 1873 budget, the major part of the income was reserved for food, for approximately 54 per cent of the income, £79 out of £150, went for the most basic of all necessities. In general, food prices did not change greatly in the second half of the century.[30] Graphs 1 and 2 illustrate this point with reference to one of the most important food items in the budget — meat. For the period 1832-92, the change in meat prices was not significant. But this is the point of view of macro-economics, which really does not capture the problem of the middle-class housewife. Her concern was with micro-economics, yearly changes. For a woman who began housekeeping in 1852, the change in meat prices would certainly seem substantial. As the graphs indicate for the years 1852-82 (with the exception of a few brief years in the mid-sixties) meat prices were rising. This produced a wide array of complaints. In the 1870s it was remarked that 'meat and farm produce has risen so as to cause serious inconvenience in most families'.[31] And apart from these serious short-run increases, the rough long-range stability of food prices meant that there was no relief in this area, where so much of the budget was consumed in compensating for increases in other costs such as rent. In this sense, food prices seemed more burdensome in the second half of the century than in the first.

The increasing cost of rent was a particular problem for many middle-class families. Rents in England doubled between 1831 and 1881.[32] The most hard-pressed by the rent increases were the city dwellers, and the middle class, with its desire for good housing, was hard hit. In 1866, a manual entitled *The Household* noted that families of £200 and £300 per year were being forced to pay as much as 20 per cent of their

Graph 1   Average Meat Prices in England, 1832-1892

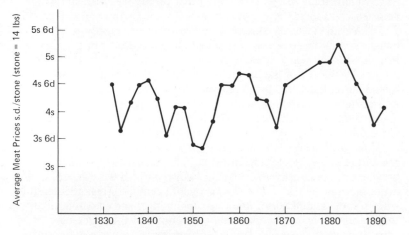

Source: *Annual Register* and *London Illustrated News,*
Augustus Sauerbeck, *Prices of Commodities During the last
Seven Years* (London, 1893), pp. 27-8.

Graph 2   Average Meat Price Range in England, 1832-1892

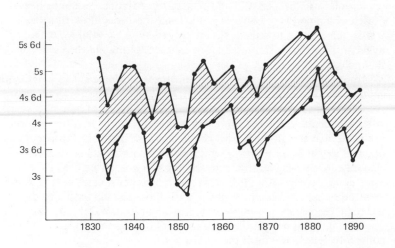

Sources: Same as Graph 1

incomes for rent alone.[33] This was the same opinion expressed by Baxter in his study in 1867. He noted that for families with an income between £100 and £300 per year, rental costs were between £20 and £50.[34] Yet the manuals continued to insist that one-eighth of the budget was all that was to be expended on rent. Because of the great increase in rents many middle-class families were forced to flee to the suburbs by the end of the century. Although they found rents reduced by the move, they were then confronted with the additional expense of transportation to and from work.[35] For many middle-class families it must have seemed like a vicious circle, escaping one expense to incur yet another.

Along with rising costs came new expenses which would in the long run define a new middle-class life stule. The middle-class woman became a prime target for advertising, which grew to the status of a major industry by the end of the nineteenth century. This reflected the woman's role as director of the household budget and encouraged her to take on new tasks as a consumer. The effects of the increased advertising were numerous. It not only made the woman more aware of the many new items available to her, but also must have added some frustration and discontentment when she could not afford the rapidly expanding array of new products for the home and family. For advertising helped convince more and more families that a number of new products were actual necessities, particularly in the area of sanitary facilities and home appliances. Middle-class women sought new ways to perform their household tasks; hence, the interest in appliances. The desire for plumbing facilities, part of what has been termed the sanitary revolution, went deeper still, and related to new concerns about health as well as the pervasive concern with cleanly respectability. In other words, the impulse to stretch the budget to buy new things was fanned by advertising, but it stemmed from concerns of middle-class women themselves.

Among the many new improvements made available in the nineteenth century for the home was piped water, hot and cold. Better drainage systems were sought. Bath tubs were added to the list of bare necessities. After mid-century, the bath tub was removed from its traditional place in the kitchen and given its own room. The cost of a bath tub depended upon its size and composition which could be quite expensive and elaborate, depending on the taste and pocketbook of the buyer. The more common galvanized tubs cost about 30s, per square foot.[36] There were a number of different types of bath tubs. The hip bath and the sitz bath, for instance, were very widely advertised. Water closets were also an important part of the sanitary revolution, although they did not come into general use until the 1880s.

Many of the home improvements were directly beneficial to the middle-class housewife, especially those for the kitchen. The open fireplace with its variety of spits and hanging hooks and the portable oven gave way to the coal burning, cast iron range. A simple open range varied in price from £3.10s. up to £7.5s., depending on its size and accessories. The 1840s saw the invention of the close range. Soon after, the famous 'kitchner' was displayed at the 1851 exhibition, but this was too expensive for the middle-class household. A close range was more reasonable. Its cost was about £5.15s.[37] For some middle-class homes there were new washing machines. The cost of a small machine was advertised about £2 − £3.[38] Since the wash of the middle-class family was done mainly in the home and the middle-class wife was responsible for most of the cooking, these appliances were becoming increasingly popular.

One important addition to the middle-class woman's home, which has been somewhat neglected, was the sewing machine. The demand for this item increased at a phenomenal rate during the second half of the century. The many advertisements and the increasing number of inquiries from women to magazines asking for information on the various makes of machines indicate its growing importance. A letter written by a woman in response to a series of articles on the sewing machine, which appeared in 1867 in the EDM, illustrated the situation. She wrote that

> Yours papers on the sewing machine, will, I think, prove
> very useful in aiding us in the purchase of a really good and
> serviceable machine . . . there is so much difficulty in
> arriving at the advantages and disadvantages of the many
> different makes.[39]

Among the many machines described in the series of articles appearing in the EDM were: the 'Grove & Baker' which sold for £9, £10, £11 and £16, 'Newton Wilson' at £8, £9.9s., £10.10s., £12.12s., and £14.14s.; Wright and Mann's 'Excelsior' at £6.6s., £7, £12.12s.; the 'Thomas' at £6, £8, £10, £15 (this manufacturer advertised an inexpensive hand model also for £5.5s.). There was also the 'Wanzer' which sold for £9, £10, £11 and £15. And of course, the most famous of all, the 'Singer' which sold for £9, £10, £14 and £15.[40] Since the middle-class woman had to make most of her own clothing and that of her children, she certainly would desire this new addition for the home.

In addition to these new items, the woman had to provide for the basic furnishings for the home. According to the *Manual of Domestic Economy*, the cost of the minimum household furnishings for a family earning £150 per year was £63.10s.;[41] almost half a year's salary. With this in mind, plus the costs of the new items listed above, it appears that the woman either had to save for many years or buy most of her furnishings and appliances on the instalment plan, which added to her ultimate expenses. The table below gives an idea of some of the new expenses encountered by the middle-class housewife in the second half of the century:

TABLE VI

Table of Expenditures for Middle-Class Household

Item	Price Range	Average Cost
Stove	£3.10s. – £7.10s.	£5.10s.
Washing Machine	£2 – £3	£2.10s.
Sewing Machine	£6 – £15	£10
Bath	30s. per sq. ft.	£3.10s.

We can now see how a single new appliance might fit into what was a tight, and probably increasingly tight, middle-class budget. Looking back over the 1873 budget plan presented in the previous chapter, it can be seen that, at most, £20 per year was reserved for appliances, furnishings, and medical expenses. According to various sources the doctor's bills and chemist costs would be a minimum of about £5. In addition, not considered in the manuals' budgets but related to health, there was life insurance, which had to be paid for out of the £20 pool as well. Insurance protection was becoming an absolute must in middle-class families, as the rising number of insurance companies and increasing number of advertisements attest. According to an insurance company's report, the average amount of insurance bought was for £445 coverage, which at the lowest premium available cost about £9 per year.[42] This left £6 for basic household furnishings. If we allow half of this money to go for new expenditures, it can be seen from the table above that it would take the housewife three and one-quarter years to save enough money to buy a sewing machine outright. In fact, most women must therefore have bought it on the gradual payment system which required that she only put down 5-7 per cent of the cost on deposit;[43] but this again meant that, with interest fees, the household budget would be burdened for about four years.

All of this is far from the conventional image of the ornamental middle-class woman. Too often, the piano has been cited as the typical new expenditure, and the image of the middle-class woman sitting at the piano is a part of the sterotype.[44] However, there were few, if any, advertisements or inquiries made for pianos in the women's magazines or general family magazines. They did appear regularly in the very fashionable press, as in the *London Illustrated News*. According to the advertisements, it seems that new pianos were out of the question for most middle-class families which is why they were not advertised in their manuals. New pianos ranged in price from £28 to £120, depending on the size and ornamentation.[45] Even second-hand pianos, according to the advertisements, started at £12 and up. Thus, it was probably more common to hear the sound of the sewing machine in the middle-class home than the piano, since any extra time the mistress could find would be spent in making her clothing. The sewing machine, the washing machine, the stove, and the bath were the type of 'luxury' items that are significant in understanding the changes in the middle-class life style. For indeed, these items were considered significant gains by women who had to cook over a hot open fire or wash and sew their clothes by hand. To emphasize grand houses, elegant carriages and horses, and lavish dinner parties as part of the typical middle-class life style is simply not realistic.

The above discussion on the actual economic situation facing the middle-class woman and the real nature of the change in her style of living helps us better to understand her continuing problems with finances, to which there really was no solution. Though she did experience rising expectations, and did desire new additions to her home, she had to be content with only the most economical and practical of novelties. The middle-class housewife was never able to free herself from money cares, for she simply did not have the means to do so. The restrictions of a narrow income in a society of rising costs and constant innovation put a great deal of strain on the woman as budget-manager. How deeply affected emotionally she was from the never-ending anxiety of money problems, plus the barrage of criticism she faced about her frivolity, is impossible to determine exactly. An article in the magazine *The Mothers' Companion*, entitled 'The Ill-Health of Women', noted that

> The problem of making both ends meet when the income is insufficient has a most pernicious effect upon women's health. The process is thoroughly disheartening and devitalizing. It gives an anxious, worn expression easy to recognize. — Those who toil so laboriously to save must of necessity, spend themselves.[46]

In the context of the dilemma of the household budget, plus the sheer physical labor involved in maintaining the apartment and the family's food and clothing, the servant question takes on new dimensions. This was the second household responsibility which women found particularly troublesome throughout the nineteenth century. As mistress of the house, it was the middle-class woman's job to hire, fire, and order the servants. In this relationship she assumed a totally new role — that of employer. Inexperience was one reason that many middle-class women found the managing of servants distressing, as noted earlier. But this was only part of the problem.

Historians have delighted in discussing the relationship of servants to the middle class, but rarely get beyond describing values and attitudes. For example, one social historian suggests that the keeping of domestic servants by the middle class

> . . . went to the very heart of the idea of class itself. The essence of middle classness was the experience of relating to other classes or orders in society. With one group, domestic servants, the middle class stood in a very special and intimate relationship; the one in fact played an essential part in defining the identity of the other.[47]

Conventionally, the domestic servant is viewed almost exclusively as a status symbol that the family had arrived socially. It is common to hear that the main distinguishing characteristic between a middle-class woman and those below her was an attitude of mind which demanded that she have at least one servant to wait upon her. In part this is true. However, historians have gone from one servant to many in defining the middle-class household in the nineteenth century. It is now assumed that the typical middle-class home was not complete until it had, at the very least, three domestics; a cook, a parlor-maid, and a nurse or housemaid.[48] This is a serious distortion of the middle-class situation. The typical middle-class home could not possibly afford to hire three domestics; it had only one servant, generally a maid-of-all-work, or to be more 'genteel,' a general servant. How historians came to define the middle-class situation as having three domestics is indeed puzzling. Even contemporaries agreed that the rule in England was the maid-of-all-work.[49] An anlysis of servants' wages and their numbers and types will prove this point.

The average yearly wage of a cook was about £20, while a parlor-maid received £20 and a nurse-housemaid about £16. Therefore, the annual expenditure for just the minimum number of domestics, as conventionally defined, was £56.[50] This would mean that families earning £100–£300 per year would have had to expend almost 20 per cent of their incomes in the highest level and more than 50 per cent on the lowest levels. This simply was not economically feasible. In order to employ these three domestics, a family had to have an annual income within the range of £400 to £500, which would put them in the upper middle class. Thus, it can be seen again that we have judged the whole middle-class situation on the basis of a purely upper middle-class model. Almost all the contemporary sources agreed that at the £300 income level, the maid-of-all-work could be employed, along with an occasional girl. Under £300 only one servant could be afforded.[51] Mrs. Warren stressed this over and over in several of her works.[52] The only servant, therefore, that the middle-class woman could keep was a maid-of-all-work, whose wage was from £9 to £14 per year.

The census data confirm further that the middle-class woman had to be content with only one servant. For example, the 1871 census listed 93,000 cooks.[53] If one allows a cook for every upper-class family — and there were, according to Baxter, about 50,000 upper-class families in all,[54] that would leave only 43,000 cooks to serve all the middle class. Since there were approximately 150,000 families in the upper middle class alone, those whose annual income was over £300, it is apparent that even in these ranks a cook was not always a part of the household. There simply were not enough cooks to serve both the aristocracy and the middle class. In terms of numbers, the only type of domestic servant which could begin to fill the needs of the more than 600,000 middle-class families who made between £100 and £300 was the general servant. The table below on the distribution of servants for the period 1851-71 illustrates this fact clearly.

TABLE VII

Domestic Servants 1851-1871

Domestic Servant	1851	1861	1871	% Increase 1851-71
General Servant	575,162	644,271	780,040	35.6
Housemaid	49,885	102,462	110,505	121.5
Housekeeper	46,648	66,406	140,836	201.9
Cooks	44,004	77,822	93,067	111.5
Nursemaids	35,937	67,785	75,491	110.1

Source: Banks, *Prosperity and Parenthood*, p. 37.

The tremendous rate of increase in just twenty years in the number of housemaids (121.5 per cent) and housekeepers (210.9 per cent), and cooks (111.5 per cent), had led some to conclude that these servants were becoming increasingly common in the middle-class home.[55] However, their numbers never approached the number of middle-class families in the upper levels alone. It may be more interesting to note that the small increase in the numbers of general servants probably did not keep pace with the growth of the central segment of the middle class, which might reflect the economic problems discussed above. There is no guarantee that every household in this group afforded a servant at all. But most undoubtedly did, even in 1871, and this brings us back to the main point. In terms of economics and in terms of availability, the one and only servant in the majority of middle-class homes employing servants was the maid-of-all-work. Yet what do we know about her?

The idealized servant maid of Victorian literature, Mary, the housemaid of Mr. Nupkins of Ipswich, or Mary of the cherry-colored ribbons who took the heart of Sam Weller in Dickens' *Pickwick Papers*, was by no means the typical servant girl in the nineteenth century. The typical servant was, in fact, the crudest of all domestic servants, certainly the least trained. She came from extreme poverty, either from a laborer's cottage, where it was no longer possible to feed or clothe her, or from the wretched slums of the city. She had no idea of what the middle class considered the ordinary habits of civilized life, let alone the refinements of cleanliness, honesty, and sobriety.[56] She was generally a very young girl. The 1871 census indicated that almost half (49.7 per cent) of the general servants were under twenty years of age. The largest percentage (about 38 per cent) were between the ages of 15 and 19.[57]

What did this mean for the middle-class mistress? The irony of the situation is again keen for the middle-class housewife, because almost all the advice on management of servants was irrelevant to her situation. For example, the frequent recommendations of minute investigation of a servant's character were not very useful, for many of the servant girls did not have character references, coming to the housewife without prior experience.

In order fully to understand the relationship between the middle-class mistress and her servant, one must realize that this relationship was very intimate and intense. It was this intimacy which accounted for many of the daily tensions. The middle-class woman, unlike her upper-class sister, had a one-to-one relationship with her maid. She had to tell the maid directly what to do. As a result the mistress became the object of much of the servant's displeasure when she did not like the work. In contrast, the upper-class woman had a housekeeper to whom she gave all her orders, which the housekeeper in turn transmitted to the various domestics. The upper-class woman rarely came into contact with the other servants, especially one as low as the maid-of-all-work. Thus she did not encounter the many problems of discipline and complaints.

One of the greatest sources of tension in the middle-class home was the work load. As was briefly noted earlier, the amount of daily menial labor involved in keeping the middle-class home was overwhelming and physically exhausting, for only two women, especially a home that had the care of at least three children, which was the norm by the end of the century. Because of the extremely heavy work load and minimum return in wages — endemic conditions in the middle-class family — many young girls were constantly changing positions, rarely spending more than a year in one home. This constant turnover created severe problems for the middle-class mistress. The housewife had to face the probability that by the time she worked out a suitable relationship with her girl, the girl would leave her for another position. Hence her problems with domestic servants was never-ending.

Servants were thus a mixed blessing in the middle-class household, necessary only because of the physical burdens of maintaining the standard of living the class had developed. Given a few additional household appliances and even a slight increase in the wage of the general servant, the middle class may have begun to abandon the employment of servants without too much regret, a transformation that became quite visible by the 1890s. But during the crucial middle decades of the nineteenth century, the problems of directing an unskilled often sulky teenaged servant must be added to the serious strain of household direction.

Notes

1. Lewis and Angus Maude, *The English Middle Classes*; and Charles Moraze, *The Triumph of the Middle Class: A Study of European Values in the Nineteenth Century* (Cleveland, 1966) deal too exclusively with values. In contrast to these studies is Adeline Daumard's *Bourgeoisie Parisienne de 1815 à 1848* (Paris, 1963), a good study of the French middle class which gets beyond values.
2. For recent discussions on birth control and women with class distinctions see Peter Stearns, *European Society in Upheaval*, 2nd ed. (New York, 1975), pp. 139-44, and Edward Shorter, 'Female Emancipation,' pp. 605-40.
3. John Foster, *Class Struggle in the Industrial Revolution*, (London, 1974).
4. In F.M.L. Thompson's *Hampstead: Building a Borough 1650-1964* (Boston, 1974) little data on behavior and outlook is offered in favor of a predominant interest in tracing building patterns themseves. Alan Armstrong in *Stability and Change in an English Country Town: A Social Study of York 1801-1851* (Cambridge, 1974), writing a more genuine social history, nevertheless confines himself to overall city statistics on marriage rates and the like; only with regard to fertility does he venture into class-specific materials, a point to which we will return.
5. *The Englishwoman's Domestic Magazine*, (June 1869), p. 326.
6. *Health and Home*, p. 107.
7. Bessie Rayner Parkes Belloc, *Essay on Woman's Work*, 2nd ed. (London, 1865), pp. 83-105.
8. Banks, *Prosperity and Parenthood*, p. 48; Best, *Mid-Victorian Britain*, p. 90; Dunbar, *Early Victorian Woman*, p. 66.
9. Banks, *Prosperity and Parenthood*, p. 101.
10. Patrick Colquhoun, *A Treatise on Indigence* (1806).
11. Daumard's *Bourgeoisie Parisienne* and Jean Lambert-Dansette, *Quelques Familles Du Patronat Textile De Lille-Armentières* (Lille, 1954) are French studies which at least touch upon these relationships.
12. R.D. Baxter, *National Income* (London, 1868).

13. The greatest difficulty with Baxter's material for this study was that he did not give the average incomes for the various occupational groups in the middle class as did Colquhoun.

14. It should be noted that Baxter's findings have been used extensively by Perkin in his work *The Origins of English Society*, and also by Eric Hobsbawm in his essay 'The Labour Aristocracy in Nineteenth Century Britain,' contained in his work *Labouring Man* (New York, 1967), pp. 321-70. This does not remove the difficulties in the source, which may have been used too uncritically, but it does add some credibility, if only for want of anything better, to its use at least as a general guideline.

15. Baxter, *National Income*, Appendix I, p. 61.

16. Ibid., p. 64.

17. The 1803 figures was reported in Perkin's *The Origin of English Society*, pp. 20-21. The 1867 figure was found in Baxter's *National Income*, Appendix I, p. 82. The £100–£300 income range may have a surprising durability even beyond this period; for example, as late as 1910 the yearly salary of an engineer in a manufacturing firm was £200; from H.A. Roberts, *Careers for University Men* (Cambridge, 1914), quoted in Sheldon Rothblott, *Revolution of the Dons*, p. 285.

18. Josephine Kamm, *Hope Deferred: Girls' Educations in English History* (London, 1965).

19. Dunbar, *Early Victorian Woman*, p. 136

20. *The English Woman's Journal* (July 1859), advertisement.

21. *The English Woman's Domestic Magazine*, Vol. V (1868), p. 109.

22. Available model budgets allowed only 12 per cent of the annual income to cover not only education costs but also servant's wage, charities, and incidental expenses. The manual *Practical Domestic Economy* noted that not until the £500 income level was there sufficient funds to educate one child (p. 407). To be sure, some middle-class families saved up, over a period of years, but their attention undoubtedly went first to sons and could rarely extend to more than one child. Few daughters, in this period, had the good fortune to be only children, as will be obvious in our later discussion of average birth rates.

23. H.C. Barnard, *A History of English Education from 1760* (London, 1961), p. 155.

24. M. Jeanne Peterson, 'The Victorian Governess: Status Incongruence in Family and Society,' in *Victorian Studies*, Vol. XIV, No. 1, pp. 7-26; also published in Vicinus's collection *Suffer and Be Still*, pp. 3-20.

25. *Census of England and Wales, 1871*, Summary Tables, Table XIX, p. xliv. Four years before the census was taken there were 150,000 families in the upper middle class alone. A family with the norm of five children, spaced two years apart, would require the service of a governess for ten years to take the education even of the eldest child well into the primary level. If we generously assume that two-thirds of the upper-middle-class families of 1867 had either passed or not yet reached their ten-year childbearing period, the remaining segment would still have used up the entire corps of governesses by itself. As the aristocracy undoubtedly had first call on most available governesses, it is apparent that there were not enough to service the upper middle class alone.

26. Peterson, 'The Victorian Governess,' pp. 11-12.

27. For a history of education in the nineteenth century see Barnard, *History of English Education*; P.W. Musgrove, *Society and Education in England Since 1800* (London, 1968); Brian Simon, *Studies in the History of Education, 1780-1870* (London, 1960).

28. Walsh, *The Manual of Domestic Economy*, (London, 1873).
29. Banks, *Prosperity and Parenthood*, pp. 66-9. Although incomes may have been rising, the principal effect was to bring more of the population into the two lower levels of the middle class. The slow rate of increase in the upper middle-class level indicates that few moved out of the central middle class. Thus the major point that follows concerning financial stringency still holds.
30. See George H. Wood, 'Real Wages and the Standard of Comfort Since 1850,' *Journal of the Royal Statistical Society*, Volume LXXII (March 1909).
31. Banks, *Prosperity and Parenthood*, pp. 66-7.
32. Ibid., p. 58.
33. *The Household: A Book of Reference Upon Subjects Relating to Domestic Economy and Home Enjoyment* (London, 1866), p. 3.
34. Baxter, *National Income*, p. 37.
35. One commuter, 'Another Happy Man,' noted that a season ticket cost him £8 in 1858; cited in Banks, *Prosperity and Parenthood*, p. 58.
36. Walsh, *Manual of Domestic Economy* (1873), p. 63.
37. The price of stoves were quoted in Beeton's *Household Management*, p. 27.
38. Ward and Lock's *Home Book*, p. 321.
39. *The Englishwoman's Domestic Magazine* (1867), p. 333.
40. Ibid., pp. 403, 485, 541, 587, 626.
41. Walsh, *Manual of Domestic Economy*, (1873), pp. 195-204.
42. The figures are from the London Assurance Corporation as reported in *Whitaker's Almanac* (1880), pp. 218-19.
43. Banks, *Prosperity and Parenthood*, p. 54.
44. Arthur Loesser, *Men, Women and Pianos: A Social History* (New York, 1954); Banks, *Prosperity and Parenthood*, p. 54.
45. Loesser, *Pianos: A Social History*, p. 259.
46. *The Mothers' Companion*, Vol. II (1888), p. 103.
47. Harrison, *Early Victorians*, p. 110.
48. Banks, *Prosperity and Parenthood*, p. 76.
49. *The Englishwoman's Domestic Magazine*, Vol. IX (1864), p. 371.
50. Charles Booth, *Life and Labour of the People in London*, Vol. VIII (London, 1896), p. 223.
51. Beeton, *Household Management*, p. 8.
52. Warren, *Managed My House on Two Hundred Pounds*, p. 55; and *Comfort for Small Incomes*, pp. 9-15.
53. *Census of England and Wales, 1871*, Summary Tables, Table XIX, p. xliv.
54. Baxter, *National Income*, p. 36.
55. Banks, *Prosperity and Parenthood*, p. 83.
56. Dunbar, *Early Victorian Woman*, pp. 49-50.
57. *Census of England and Wales, 1871*, Summary Tables, Table XIX, p. xliv.

PART II

THE INNER WOMAN

4 THE STRUGGLE FOR BETTER HEALTH

The outer dimensions of the middle-class woman's life as homemaker lead us now to the intimate aspects of her life — to the inner woman. One of the most important features of this personal life was physical health. A woman's life, more than a man's, is marked dramatically by such physical developments as puberty, pregnancy and menopause. Yet we know virtually nothing about the health of the middle-class woman in the nineteenth century. Historians have either assumed a rather regular improvement, from the vantage point of definable advances in medical knowledge, or they have neglected key aspects of a woman's life, such as pregnancy, assuming these are relative constants in the female experience and thus not susceptible to analysis. In the following chapters we will see that not only were there substantial changes in the personal health of women but also that middle-class women were the prime movers for these changes. The middle-class woman applied her new mentality to her personal life as well as to her role as homemaker, and in many instances with more success. In coping with her personal problems she demonstrated again an openness to change, a desire for rationalization and an effort, appropriate in a utilitarian century, to maximize pleasure and minimize pain. Through her efforts to gain control of her personal being, the middle-class woman was able to express most successfully her new self-image. Though the new mentality was most clearly visible in the field of health, it extended to related activities such as child-rearing and sexual enjoyment. Many strands of the new personal outlook united in the development of birth control, a familiar monument to the Victorian middle class which now requires reassessment as we see women as active moulders of their personal situation.

But we begin with health, because improvement here was essential to greater activity in other areas. Advances in women's health were set by two nineteenth-century developments. One was a declining sense of fatalism. Middle-class women were the first large group to establish a modern outlook toward life and death; they no longer tolerated pain and early death as uncontrollable aspects of existence, for both could and should be conquered. They demanded better health for themselves and, relatedly, for their children, who were increasingly seen as expressions of themselves and thus deserving the right to life. They were the leaders in the campaigns of the nineteenth century against the high traditional rates of maternal and infant mortality, and in practice they experimented with a variety of new methods to cope with the problems of childbirth, not only the omnipresent danger of death but also pain.

Accompanying the new outlook was the growing influence of science, most specifically in the increased interaction between middle-class women and doctors.[1] As the medical histories note, nineteenth-century England witnessed the professionalization of doctors, along with the expansion of the medical corps. The number of doctors increased by 53 per cent in the thirty years after 1861, from 17,300 to 26,500.[2] The professionalization process involved such laws as the 1858 Medical Registration Act which set up a General Register for licensed doctors and established a General Medical Council which determined qualifications for registration. Specialization was another aspect of the professionalization process, and it is here that medical advances bore most directly on women. In the nineteenth century, obstetric and gynecological medicine developed as distinct specialities, bringing forth important advances in the treatment of a number of female health problems. However, fields such as obstetrics and gynecology were not just expressions of the professionalization process but fundamentally its product; that is, the new medical fields were designed, in the first instance, in the interest of doctors, who needed new jobs and new claims to knowledge, and only somewhat later benefited the presumed clientele. This means that the gap between what was possible in terms of medical knowledge in obstetrics and gynecology and what was actually made available to middle-class women was filled only slowly, while common problems might be neglected in favor of treatment of rarer, if dramatic, disorders.

In the nineteenth century problems of women's health gained unprecedented attention from the medical profession. The number of books written specifically on the subject, such as Dr. Fleetwood Churchill's *On the Diseases of Women*,[3] proliferated by mid-century. Furthermore, doctors began to contribute regularly to women's magazines. More women's hospitals were founded to provide special care, and these also offered a fertile field for experimentation on women's health problems and thus fed the new specialization further. It was mainly from these centers, through the efforts of a few pioneering individuals such as James Young Simpson and Robert Lawson Tait, that the important new theories, technological developments and surgical procedures were elaborated.

By the middle of the century the gynecologists had developed their own armamentarium. Early in the century the vaginal speculum was reintroduced into England, largely due to the efforts of Simpson. This instrument allowed the doctor to make a visual examination of the vagina, for prior to this his only method of examination had been manual. Between 1800 and 1900 four hundred different vaginal speculums were developed. Soon after the speculum, the curette, the dilator, and the uterine sound were added. In the second half of the

63

century some of the most important surgical techniques were perfected; collectively their development has been characterized as the birth of modern gynecology. The most often-quoted surgical advances were the successful performance of ovariotomies, the repair of vesico-vaginal fistula (a rupture), the removal of fibroids from the uterus, the removal of diseased Fallopian tubes, and the handling of ectopic pregnancy. The last two procedures owe their success to Britain's outstanding gynecologist, Robert Lawson Tait. As most medical histories note, these five operative procedures were the really great accomplishments of nineteenth-century gynecology.[4]

Prior to the surgical advances there was no hope for women who suffered from the malfunctions peculiar to their sex. Occasionally an ovarian cyst might be tapped, but this offered little comfort and no help, for the cyst would continue to fill with fluid. In one case, for example, the attending physician reported removing 140 gallons of fluid from a single ovary.[5] Most women endured the pain of the cyst rather than face the immediate consequence of the earlier ovariotomies — death.

Along with the meteoric rise of surgery, there were the non-surgical innovations and crazes in gynecological therapy; for example, the use of electricity and of massage, the excessive use of medicated tampons, the application of various pastes and medicines and the use of a fantastic variety of pessaries.[6] In 1864, it was reported that about 123 different kinds of pessaries were developed, embracing the very simple plug to a patent threshing machine which could only be worn with a very large hoop.[7] Most of the non-surgical methods were of little value but they indicate the interest that women's medicine had engendered.

At first sight the list of nineteenth-century developments in gynecology is impressive. It is certainly not surprising that many medical histories conclude that these changes contributed materially to the health of nineteenth-century women. But this conclusion fails to distinguish clearly between the interests of the doctor and the interests of the patient, which is the greatest fault of most medical histories to date. From the viewpoint of the doctor, the advances were important developments to the profession. But from the viewpoint of the patient, which is the major concern of this study, none of these changes has any practical significance until such a time as they contribute to preservation of health or recovery from illness. There is often a substantial interval of time between acquisition of new knowledge and the possibility of any demonstrable benefit to the patient. Thus it is not appropriate to accept changes in medical education and institutions as evidence of the immediate effectiveness of medical effort.

In fact the anticipations developed by middle-class women from their declining sense of fatalism were not readily met by existing medical practice. The lack of a neat mesh between women's interests and actual changes in health derives from many factors. Medical knowledge, though advancing, was still primitive in many ways, quite apart from failures to apply widely what was known. Women were limited in their ability to call in the best practitioners. In fact something of a vicious circle existed. Many doctors saw only women in the throes of extreme physical problems; lesser difficulties were not called to their attention. But doctors' inability to offer aid to more common health problems limited women's interest in using them, for their use could involve sacrifice.

When, in fact, did Victorian women see doctors? Doctors were relatively new to the middle class and their expansion in numbers should not becloud this fact. There is no evidence that middle-class women turned to them quickly for minor ailments. The practical reasons were numerous. Chaperonage was one. A woman would not readily see a doctor unless accompanied by another female. This practice was common to the end of the century as indicated by Dr. Allbutt's warnings that:

> ... whenever it is necessary for an examination of a young girl
> to be made, the girl's mother or some elderly female should
> remain in the room during the examination. This caution
> must never be omitted, and it is always proposed by the doctor.
> The same rule holds good for grown-up women whether
> married or single. Observance of this practice would save much
> sorrow to both patient and doctor.[8]

Second, and more important, was sheer economic limitation. Most middle-class families could not afford the luxury of consulting doctors frequently. As we saw earlier, £10-£20 a year were allocated to the very general category of family medical expenses, amusements, and sometimes furnishings, with £5 assumed a normal minimum for all health costs including drugs. With doctors' fees about £1 per visit this left some margin for consultation over particular problems such as pregnancy, but not much in normal years for a woman of a family of five or more with some desire for entertainment, new appliances and the like. A cheaper alternative would be welcomed.

One alternative was the new health manuals written by doctors specifically for the new middle class — well within their economic range and catering to their growing interest in health. They promised to provide women with all the information necessary for their personal health care; Dr. Fennings' manual,[9] for example, offered women the secrets of science for those critical periods in life, along with information on how to feed, clothe, and educate their children. A special added attraction was a section on his miracle cures for female maladies. Manuals of this sort were widely advertised in the popular women's magazines. Yet, most of them offered only grandiose claims, for they contained little concrete advice beyond the very simple rules on moderation in diet, exercise and the importance of fresh air. As in the case the domestic manuals, many of the health guides increased anxieties more than they allayed them. Some doctors, even those who sought a large audience, were surprisingly hostile to modern urban civilization, and they took pleasure in finding much of the presumed behavior of middle-class women unnatural. The myth of the idle Victorian woman was dominant here. Many doctors claimed that the nineteenth-century middle-class woman's health had deteriorated, and other publicists followed suit, agreeing also that the blame rested squarely on the effete shoulders of women themselves. The author of *The English Matron* set forth the following opinion about her subjects:

> ... we English matrons are far more feeble a race than our grandmothers or even our mothers were ... Witness our easily excited feelings, witness our late hours of rising, our sofas and easy chairs, our useless days and dissipated nights! Witness our pallid faces, our forms, sometimes attenuated and repulsive while yet in early life, age marching, not creeping, on before his time; or witness our over-fed and over expanded forms, enfeebled by indolence, and suffering the worst species of debility – the debility of *fat*.[10]

A good illustration of this belief that middle-class women's life style was the source of their ill health involves the debate over fashion, which loomed large, particularly in the medical columns of the women's periodicals. The lament was constant: women were sacrificing their health for fashion's sake. A common complaint was that consumption resulted from low-cut dresses and thin shoes. More popular still, on the subject of health *v*. fashion, was tight lacing and its evils, and this also drew the widest response from readers. The worst aspects of tight lacing were held to be consumption and breast tumors; the practice was also blamed for flattening nipples and preventing women from nursing their children. This kind of comment had little relevance, which is one reason that tight-lacing continued for many years. The fact was that despite the durable fashion most women already had sense enough not to tie their stays tightly; as Dr. Alice Kerr indicated in her lectures on female health problems, 'I am not going to say anything about tight stays because I never yet met anyone who wore them tight.'[11] Overall, the medical manuals pandered to worries about health rather than offering realistic remedies. Many of the causes of ill-health they attacked were superficial. Remedies to actual disease were general, little more than a formalization of tradition; hence a purgative, the wonder-cure of the century, was recommended for almost every ailment. The manuals drew an audience for reasons of low cost and claims to science, but they were not even a first step toward a really new approach to health.

A second cheap alternative widely used by middle-class women was patent medicines. Sale of these cure-alls became a booming business in the nineteenth century, reaching a far wider audience than ever before mainly by means of advertising in the cheap press. A typical wonder drug was Frompton's Bill of Health, which claimed

> . . . long time efficiency for correcting all disorders of the
> Stomach and Bowels, the common symptoms of which are
> costiveness, Flatulency, Spasms, loss of appetite, sick headache,
> Giddiness, Sense of Fullness after meals . . . for FEMALES
> these pills are most truly excellent, removing all obstructions
> and distressing headaches, so very prevalent with the sex,
> Depression of Spirits, Dullness of Sight, Nervous Affliction,
> Blotches, Pimples, Sallowness of the Skin, and gives a healthy
> jewel-like bloom to the complexion.[12]

In essence this panacea was nothing more than a purgative.

Strong warnings were issued against these quack medicines, often in the very periodicals that advertised them, yet middle-class women continued to rely on self-proclaimed wonder drugs. The cost element was most attractive. For one to two shillings a woman could buy a remedy to cure any and all of her common complaints. The cost of Frompton's Bill of Health, for example, was 1s.1½d. Beyond this, the quack drugs were in a sense able to appeal to the best of two worlds, the old and the new. Many of them reproduced or imitated what the middle-class woman's mother or grandmother used before her. But more important for nineteenth-century quackery was the new claim to scientific prowess.

By applying some of the newest discoveries in scientific knowledge and an esoteric terminology, nineteenth-century quackery claimed for itself a very attractive aura of modernity and authenticity which specifically appealed to the new mentality of the middle class. The many bogus testimonials from doctors confirmed further a scientific credibility. One of the famous King Quacks was James Morrison, 'The Hygeist,' who produced the famous Morrison's Pill, which taken with a glass of lemonade cured everything and made Morrison a fortune.[13] The cure-all remedies became more absurd and fantastic as the century progressed. The 1880s offered, for example, the renowned Harness World Famous Electropathic Belts. This device in some way or other was to apply the advantages of electricity to cure all ailments. The ads guaranteed to ladies cures for any form of weakness (this was a euphemism for sexual problems), 'Hysteria, Sleeplessness, Neuralgia, Indigestion, Constipation, Spasms, Rheumatic and Nervous Afflications, Irregularities of the System.' Along with the belt came a pamphlet on the *Diseases of Women* issued by Mr. C.F. Harness, Consulting

Electrician to the Medical Battery Company, Ltd., while Dr. Anna Kingsfor provided a testimonial for the ad itself, recommending the value of the book especially.[14]

We have come some way from the most obvious strand in the history of nineteenth-century medicine, the development of new medical knowledge, but some way also toward explaining why knowledge and actual health were slow to interact. Yet even in their zeal for manuals and patent medicines, middle-class women showed their own new eagerness to cure what had been previously left to purely traditional remedies. The same interest would bring women to doctors directly. There is no question that in cases of particularly definable problems of health such as pregnancy and in instances of severe illness, middle-class women increasingly sought the services of doctors. Later we will discuss more precisely the pattern of treatment concerning pregnancy and child-bearing. But in other cases also a pattern of consultation developed gradually and undoubtedly helped support the rapid growth in the number of physicians during the nineteenth century. In the long run doctors were the logical answer to the middle-class woman's increased desire for self-improvement and self-control. However, for the period under investigation, this relationship was just beginning and its benefits were rather limited. Even when women went to doctors they might find little gain, for use of doctors increased infinitely more rapidly than women's health improved. Indeed, this gap between anticipation and reality provides a useful perspective as to the actual conditions of middle-class women's health in the nineteenth century.

An overall assessment of middle-class women's health must recognize two significant factors. First, their condition was not as far from traditional and popular levels as one might imagine. The differential in incomes between the middle class and the working class was not sufficient to revolutionize this particular aspect of the middle-class women's personal being. This can be seen by looking at female mortality rates among middle-class women, which were not markedly lower than those of her working-class sisters. The rate of female mortality in the middle-class community of Camberwell,[15] for example, was not significantly lower than that of London or England as a whole and it long remained just as stubbornly high. Graph 3 illustrates these points. In Camberwell, female mortality did not begin to decline until after the 1880s. Also, middle-class women suffered the same pattern of fatal diseases. As late as the 1880s and 1890s 3.6 per cent of Camberwell's female population died annually from diseases of the respiratory organs, which was similarly the largest single cause of death for women throughout the century.[16] This is not to argue that middle-class health was fully as bad as that of workers, particularly at the end of the century; indeed improvement forms the basis of our second main

68

Graph 3   Female Mortality Rates: Camberwell, London, England, 1851-1871.

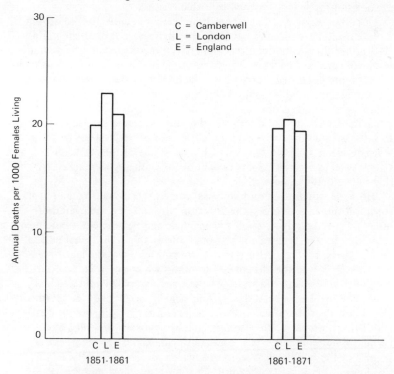

Source: Annual Report of the Registrar General, Vol. XVII, 1884-85 p.1 XXIII, 2, 63, Vol. XXIII-I, 1895, p. 193.

conclusion. But middle-class health too started from a low traditional base; and like workers, the class found it difficult to counter some of the health problems aggravated by urbanization.

Our second point is that where improvements of health did devlop they derived more often from the higher living standard of the middle class rather than from the direct benefits of medical science. The middle-class woman's new concern for greater cleanliness in the home might do her far more good than her visits to the doctor. Tuberculosis, though remaining a major killer, did recede slightly among women in Camberwell, in terms of deaths per 1000, in comparison to London rates, by the 1870s. Yet doctors had no new remedies to propose for this disease, and the women's specialists did not pretend to treat it at all. Warmer, cleaner, and less crowded homes — one of the marks of Camberwell as a middle-class community — probably accounted for the slight edge that Camberwell developed.

Thus the situation of middle-class women was ironic. Women groped for improvements; doctors, the solution why seized upon (whether directly, or indirectly through the manuals and new patent medicines) offered at best an ambivalent response during this transitional period. As we have seen, the victim was the woman. Why was the lag so persistent? Part of the answer lies in things we know already about the middle-class woman's life style. The average day of the middle-class housewife involved a great deal of physical labor. Her new concern for cleanliness drove her up and down stairs constantly, along with dusting and lifting quite heavy furnishings, preparing meals, shopping and caring for her children. As a result physical exhaustion could easily be part of the middle-class woman's health problems, and it certainly was her most common complaint. Furthermore, most middle-class women spent their entire day indoors in rooms that were never properly ventilated. Living on a tight budget, the middle-class woman was forced to conserve fuel, so to maximize the heat from her fires she made her home as airtight as possible. A common practice was to block vents in order to save on fuel bills. Windows were draped and shuttered, keeping out sunlight and fresh air in order to retain the heat. Open windows also meant damage to the rugs and furnishings and more dirt to clean, thus another reason to avoid proper ventilation. Since the major source of fuel in middle-class homes was coal, the woman was constantly exposed to these noxious fumes. Practices such as these limited her efforts at better health. They remind us how closely the middle class was tied to general urban conditions and also how in their effort to gain distinctive standards of life, Victorian women might strain themselves through overwork and rigorous budgets.

Obviously another reason for the lag in health standards was that women often went to doctors only after it was too late, as noted earlier. Doctors confronting patients in the advanced stages of illness had little to render other than pain killers.

But women were not entirely to blame. The British medical profession was generally conservative and failed to accept innovations in the field of obstetrics and gynecology. One example of this reluctance to change can be seen in the debate over the use of the vaginal speculum. Here was an instrument that greatly benefited doctors in examination of women suffering from vaginal disorders or just determining more precisely the conditions of pregnancy. Yet the objections to this method of examination were loudest from the medical profession itself. On the extreme side of the defense was Dr. Robert Carter, in writing the following:

> ... no one who has realized the amount of moral evil wrought in girls ... whose purient desires have been increased by Indian hemp and partially gratified by medical manipulation, can deny that the remedy is worse than the disease. I have ... seen young unmarried women, of the middle class of society, reduced by the constant use of the speculum, to the mental and moral condition of prostitutes, seeking to give themselves the same indulgence by the practice of solitary vice, and asking every medical practitioner ... to institute an examination of the sexual organs.[17]

Dr. Fleetwood Churchill's objections were more representative of the opposition's point of view. He found the speculum to be offensive since it required such great exposure of the female. He felt also that it offered less knowledge than examination by the finger.[18]

This brings us to a substantive problem for the transitional period. The actual level of medical knowledge about women's bodily functions was minimal for the greater part of the nineteenth century. Surgical achievements aside, and particularly among the ordinary practitioners, gynecology and obstetrics had yet to make major strides. The functions of the ovaries and fallopian tubes were not even vaguely known.[19] Though menstrual disorders were considered important there was incomplete understanding of the functions of the menstrual cycle. As late as the 1880s, it was described in an article in the *British Medical Journal* as 'an accident and incidental phenomena.'[20] Even among the specialists on women's health there was serious lack of knowledge. The consequences of this were that many theories and practices were used which were totally ineffective. Nineteenth-century gynecology was greatly limited by its approach, which involved an eternal search for the universal answer to each and every female disorder. With the introduction of the speculum the focus was on the uterus as being the cause of all female ills. In another phase of development gynecologists contended that all female problems were a matter of disorders of the menstrual cycle.[21] Even the surgical advances, although noteworthy, were of little significance until the end of the century. In 1872, the *British Medical Journal* published its findings of a survey on the number of ovariotomies performed in the leading London hospitals. The report indicated the limitedness of surgical treatments. Up in 1866, St. Bartholomew's, Middlesex, King's College, St. George, University College and Guy's hospital reported a total of 73 ovariotomies, in 51 of which the patient died.[22] One can see that ovariotomies constituted a rare surgical procedure, as they should have been at that time. They were performed only on emaciated and debilitated women suffering from huge cysts. Women who were otherwise healthy were rarely subjected to the risk of the operation. The figures on ovariotomies probably hold true for other surgical treatments. In addition it should be realized that uterine disorders were not common health problems for most women. The advances made by the pioneers helped the gynecologists and obstetricians gain respectability and prestige in the field of medicine but in reality offered little for the average woman of any social class.

Thus the conservatism of doctors plus their autonomous drive for professionalization limited greatly their contribution to the overall health of middle-class women. The irony of the situation could only enhance the anxiety of the middle-class woman. Her declining sense of fatalism, her growing need for more self-control plus the grand claims made by the medical profession — both professionals and quacks — led her to believe that real and immediate improvements were possible. But all she saw was the continued high rate of female mortality. Yet irony should not be pushed too far. Doctors did provide services to the woman even though at first the results were ambiguous. Childbirth is a case in point and a vital one because it loomed so large in the lives of middle-class women. As part of the new efforts to enhance their personal well-being women sought to improve the handling of pregnancy, delivery and post-natal care and sought the services of the doctor. Middle-class women and doctors were able to make dramatic changes in the pattern of treatment of childbirth. Yet the problems of transition were fully present in this area as elsewhere. The interaction of doctors and middle-class women was at times successful, at times tense and anxiety-ridden, and at times tragic in its consequences.

Notes

1. This is not to ignore the fact that from the eighteenth century and later upper-middle-class women used doctors. But their use often tended toward the recreational and faddish; middle-class medical concern developed separately and obviously had to be confined to immediate and fundamental health problems.
2. The census findings were reported in Booth's *Life and Labour* (Volume VIII).
3. Dr. Fleetwood Churchill *On the Diseases of Women: Including Those of Pregnancy and Childbed* (Philadelphia 1857).
4. Harvey Graham, *Eternal Eve: The Mysteries of Birth and the Customs that Surround it* (London, 1960), p. 274.
5. Churchill, *Diseases of Women*, p. 408.
6. James V. Ricci, *One Hundred Years of Gynaecology 1800-1900* (Philadelphia, 1945), p. 47.
7. Graham, *Eternal Eve*, p. 260.
8. Dr. Henry Albert Allbutt, *The Wife's Handbook: How a Woman Should Order Herself During Pregnancy, in the Lying-In Room, and After Delivery with Hints on the Management of the Baby and Other Matters of Importance Necessary to be Known by Married Women* (London, 1886), pp. 51-2.
9. Dr. Alfred Fennings, *Every Mother's Book: of the Child's Best Doctor* (Cowes, 1856).
10. *The English Matron* [by the author of *The English Gentlewoman*] (London, 1846), pp. 133-4.
11. Dr. Alice Kerr, 'Lectures to Women,' *Womanhood*, No. 3 (Manchester, 1884), p. 10.
12. *The Ladies's Journal – A Newspaper of Fashion, Literature, Music and Variety* (1847), advertisement.
13. Burton, *Pageant of Early Victorian England*, p. 208.
14. *The Queen*, Vol. XVI (1884), p.ii.
15. See Appendix for definition of Camberwell as middle-class.
16. *Annual Registrar's General's Report of Birth, Death, Marriages*, Vol. XXIII-I (1895), p. 123.
17. Robert Brudnell Carter, *On the Pathology and Treatment of Hysteria* (London, 1853), p. 69.
18. Churchill, *Diseases of Women*, p. 29.
19. An exact knowledge of ovarian function was not formulated until the late 1890s. Throughout most of the nineteenth century there was much confusion concerning the relationship between menstruation, ovulation, and conception. The first modern concept of menstruation began with the work of E. Knauer in 1896. A complete understanding of the physiology of menstruation had to wait until the hormonic estrogen was isolated from the human ovarian follicle in the 1920s. Graham, *Eternal Eve*, p. 316.
20. Ibid., P. 267.
21. Dr. Samuel Ashwell, *A Practical Treatise on the Diseases Peculiar to Women* (London, 1844), p. 23; Dr. S. Mason, *The Philosophy of Female Health: Being an Enquiry with its Connextion with Observations on the Nature, Causes and Treatments of Female Disorders in General* (London, 1845).
22. Graham, *Eternal Eve*, p. 267

5 THE DYNAMICS OF VICTORIAN MOTHERHOOD

Motherhood was a vital part of the lives of middle-class wives in Victorian England, but very few studies have treated the phenomenon and none has dealt with the most important perspective on the subject, the viewpoint of the mother herself. The function of bearing children has long been considered part of nature's plan and therefore either inconsequential or, at least, because of its fundamentally unchanging nature, not susceptible to historical analysis. Yet middle-class women in the nineteenth century who became mothers did have some distinctive attitudes toward motherhood and were groping for some new approaches. With them, and doubtless with many other groups of women in the past, motherhood did have a history.

Victorian wives were, among other things, constantly told that motherhood was their noblest function. Historians[1] have often dealt with this and it is an important aspect of the subject, for it is not unrealistic to assume that, so often warned of its significance, Victorian wives approached motherhood with more than usual awe. But the significance of their role as mothers lies far deeper than the reigning culture might indicate. No other function so completely captured the woman's emotions or so completely involved her physical being. Both aspects deserve attention, but in this chapter we begin with the physical act of giving birth. Here we find repeated some of the ironies of the general health experience of middle-class women in this period. There was new medical treatment available; women did seek new ways of dealing with childbirth and pregnancy. But the facts of giving birth changed more slowly. The result was considerable risk and at best great fatigue, and these physical facts were in turn to color the emotional approach to the child.

Almost all middle-class married women experienced pregnancy at least once, save where sterility prevented, and most became pregnant four or five times during their lives. The role of mother was seriously complicated by the fact that the middle-class woman usually gave birth to her first child within the initial year of marriage. Ansell's study on the upper and professional classes reports the following statistics on the interval between the marriage of the parents and the birth of the first child.[2]

TABLE VIII

Relationship Between Marriage and First Birth

No. of Cases	Interval Between Marriage & Birth
8811	10.18 months
1047	10.77 months
7705	11.33 months
7575	11.48 months
8796	11.75 months
7745	11.94 months
5724	12.18 months
4379	13.13 months

Thus out of 51,582 cases reported, 42,479 or more than 80 per cent recorded the birth of a child within the first year of marriage. Hence the woman was confronted with her most difficult role before she was able to cope with her other household responsibilities. In her book, *How I Managed My House on Two Hundred Pounds*, Eliza Warren complained of this very problem: 'My children were around me before I had devised any certain method of managing my household affairs.'[3] Mothers were advised to prepare their daughters that no sooner were they married than they would be pregnant.[4]

The Victorian woman would spend an important period of her life bearing children. Nineteenth-century doctors began to urge her to end her childbearing years at age 32 or 33. It was considered unwise for a woman at that time to allow herself to become pregnant after 35.[5] This recommendation seems to reflect the general pattern. As was noted earlier, the majority of middle-class women married between the ages of 20 and 25.[6] The years of childbearing averaged about 13.7 years in the beginning of the century and declined slightly in the later part of the century to an average of 12.4 years.[7] Thus particularly in the first half of the nineteenth century, more than a quarter of the Victorian woman's life was spent in either pregnancy or in nursing and recovery from pregnancy.[8]

For this very reason the concept of motherhood had to change; the declining sense of fatalism was intensively applied to the process of birth, while the role of medical developments was most specifically demonstrated by the growing use of doctors instead of midwives.

In the nineteenth century pregnancy was for the first time seriously discussed, though its profound complexities were just beginning to be perceived. The intense effects it had on the woman's personal being, and the intimate and vital relationship between mother and child were

75

both coming to be realized in a new and more explicit fashion. Maternal mortality and infant mortality were no longer quietly accepted as part of a divine plan. The growing emphasis in the nineteenth century was that through proper measures one could control this process of nature and improve upon it. The decline in fatalism was expressed early in the forties in an article in the *Magazine of Domestic Economy*. It stated that

> No one who has reflected upon the subject, and certainly no one who has a practical acquaintance with it, will contend that the annual deaths of 3000 women in childbirth, and of 13,350 boys and 9,740 girls in the first month after delivery, or the suffering and deformity of those who escape with life, are natural and inevitable. Admit that the lives of a thousand, or even a hundred − or of one hundred of those mothers could be saved − and that many more might be rescued from injuries and pains which disable, or never leave them; and assuredly, no apathy, no false sentiment of delicacy, will prevent those who have the public health at heart from giving the subject the most attentive consideration.[9]

The growing concern over motherhood was very apparent in the sudden mass of books which began to flood the market; examples include Dr. Bull's *Hints to Mothers*[10] which first appeared in 1833 and quickly went through fourteen editions with yet another edition in 1877, Dr. Conquest's *Letters to a Mother*[11] and Dr. Allbutt's *The Wife's Handbook*, and *Every Mother's Handbook*.[12] In addition to the hundreds of manuals published there were also periodicals produced expressly for the mother and her particular problems; for example, *The British Mother's Magazine*, and *The Mother's Friend*,[13] which ran from 1848 to 1895. New organizations were formed as well, such as the *London Maternal Association*, which were designed to bring mothers together to discuss their common experiences.

This growing concern and demand for information on the most basic aspects of motherhood suggests that the Victorian middle-class woman did not find motherhood as natural to her as it has been traditionally imagined. Many women obviously found their instinctive qualities to be insufficient. The Victorian woman seriously questioned her capabilities to fulfill her most natural of functions − motherhood. Her insecurity, or at least her sense of anxiety about her condition, was accentuated by most of the new manuals. In this field, too, manuals made their mark by capitalizing on new anxieties.

The theme most often developed was that the health of the mother-to-be and the life and health of the baby were dependent in great part on the woman and her manner of living. It was now her responsibility whether she herself lived or died or suffered and whether her baby lived or died, or was born with disabilities.

This theme was not necessarily new in popular culture, but there is no question that in the nineteenth century the woman's responsibility as a mother was more widely manifested than in any previous period because of the ever-expanding range of the press, and her responsibility as opposed to nature's role was more heavily emphasized than in any earlier period. Thus in a sense the Victorian woman was caught in a vicious circle; she was anxious about her health and the health of her unborn baby, she sought advice, but for the most part all the advice did was to confirm all her anxieties while offering very little in the way of constructive advice.

The most dramatic change in motherhood in the nineteenth century, which reflected strongly the concept of control over the process, involved the interaction of women and the medical profession. We have already noted the growing concern in the medical profession for the particular problems of women's health, most obviously through definition of the fields of gynecology and obstetrics. In fact, in terms of formal medical history, obstetrics developed and was recognized as a field worthy of specialization some time before gynecology. This followed rather obviously from the frequency of pregnancy, which gave the field of obstetrics a very wide market to explore and expand among women. In contrast, gynecology dealt more specifically with the uncommon in women, with disorders that did not have the same incidence. In addition, we must recall that gynecology was closely associated with surgery; it was not until 1929 that there was a break between general surgery and gynecology and a closer connection between obstetrics and gynecology.[14] Obstetrics, then, had a more direct bearing on nineteenth-century women than did female medicine in general. But while this means that it must be given serious consideration in the history of middle-class women, it makes its failures all the more ironic.

The growth of obstetrics in the medical profession in the nineteenth century was substantial. Early in the century, the medical profession recognised the importance of a knowledge of midwifery for the practice of medicine. In 1835, attendance at a course of lectures on midwifery was necessary to obtain the qualification of the Royal College of Surgeons and the Society of Apothecaries. In 1841, a knowledge of midwifery was required for the MB or MD degree at London University. Cambridge followed suit in 1859 and Oxford in 1860.[15] The following table lists the necessary requirements from several institutions as recorded by the end of the century:

TABLE IX

Obstetric Instructions Required

Name of Examining Body	Lectures Required on Midwifery	Clinical Instruc. at Maternity Hosp.	No. of Confinements To be Attended
Royal College of Physicians & Surgeons of England	3 months	3 months	20
Society of Apothecaries, London	3 months	3 months	20
Univ. of London	1 course	–	20
Univ. of Cambridge	1 course	–	20
Univ. of Durham	3 months	3 months	20
Victoria University	6 months	3 months	20

Source: Report from the Select Committee on Midwives' Registration (June, 1892), p. 137.

A result of the new concern with obstetrics and the increase in training was that more and more women began to call upon the services of the doctor to attend her during her confinement. Prior to the nineteenth century, midwifery was an exclusively female domain, heavily guarded by tradition and prejudices. The conditions of midwifery were for centuries appalling. Only in the eighteenth century was any requirement made for the practice of midwifery. Known as a Bishop's License, it amounted to very little in reality. In order to obtain a Bishop's License the woman had to be recommended by a few matrons, take a formal oath, and pay a fee of 18s.4d. The oath stated that the would-be midwife foreswore child substitution, abortion, sorcery, and over-charging – all very common practices. The Bishop's License in no manner guaranteed skill. No training or examination was required.[16] There were sporadic attempts to reform the practice in the eighteenth century; for example, Mrs. Stone, in her work *A Complete Practice of Midwifery* pleaded for a system of apprenticeship for midwives.[17] However, all failed.

The demand for reform and criticism of the practice of midwifery continued into the nineteenth century; for example, the *Fifth Annual Report of the Registrar General* (1842) observed that

A large proportion of the 500,000 English women who lying-in every year and have any attendance at all, are attended by midwives, who, from one cause or other, probably delicacy of the national manners in point of this kind, receive no regular preliminary instruction in anatomy and other matters, some knowledge of which a glance at the causes of death in child-birth will show is indispensable in many emergencies. It is true that a medical man can be called in where the danger is imminent; but to discover danger, a knowledge of its source is required; and those who have come in contact with mid-wives, or 'monthly nurses' are well aware that ignorance does not diminish their self-confidence.[18]

In 1858, at the first meeting of the Obstetrical Society, Dr. Amand Routh proposed compulsory training for midwives. The Society pressed for government support of a program that would provide this, but they failed to win out until after 1900. However, in 1872 they went ahead on their own and set up a board of examiners which issued a certificate of competency known as the LOS.[19]

The attacks against the midwife were at times quite severe. There were incidents of criminal proceedings against them for causing the death of women; for example in 1875 three deaths were linked to one Elizabeth Marsden and she was found guilty and imprisoned for six weeks.[20]

No doubt the impact of this criticism played some part in the growing substitution of doctors for midwives. There are some additional questions of motivation, which can only be suggested here. The growth and professionalization of trained doctors were an obvious source of attack on the midwives. But did middle-class women themselves decide to seek new treatment? Were they active agents in the transformation, or were they mainly acted upon by advice from the outside? Certainly the rise of obstetrics corresponds to women's desire to be better mothers, but the nature of the transformation is difficult to determine. In fact we have no direct data as to how many women were attended by midwives and how many by doctors.

No precise information is available on the actual number of midwives. This was largely due to the lack of registration and also to the confusing system of classification of midwives in the nineteenth-century census returns. As was mentioned earlier, sometimes midwives were referred to as monthly nurses, and in the census returns there is no breakdown as to specific types of nurses. Monthly nurses, wet-nurses, nannies, were all listed as nurse. Therefore it is impossible to estimate the precise number of midwives. This was quite evident from the proceedings of the Committee in 1892. It noted that in the 1881 census there were only 2,646 midwives listed, but the number really practising was thought to be very much in excess of that figure. How much in excess is the problem. According to one witness, who supported the need for registration of midwives, there were as many as 20,000. Dr. Rentoul, a leading spokesman for the opposition to the registration, noted that there were only about 1000 trained midwives but admitted that the number practising was probably 12,600. Another supporter thought that about three-quarters of the labors in England were attended by midwives. Dr. Rentoul, for whom precision seemed no virtue, proposed with certainty that there were many more women attended by men than was believed to be the case.[21]

However, even if one assumes that the advocates of registration were correct and that half to three-quarters of the births were attended by mid-wives, it is still very probable that most middle-class women were attended by male practitioners. In 1891, there were 914,157 births[22] and if three-quarters were attended by midwives, the extreme position, that would leave 228,500 women who were attended by doctors. Certainly the number of middle-class women who gave birth that year did not exceed this number by very much, if at all.

A more precise method of determining the question of doctors versus midwives is through economics. According to almost all the witnesses to the committee (there was almost total agreement), the primary inducement to call upon a midwife was purely economic. On this point there is direct evidence to support the position that middle-class women used doctors rather than midwives. According to several different witnesses midwives' fees ranged from 2s.6d. to 10s. The lower fee was for the untrained midwife. The upper fee, which was noted to be exceptional, was for a trained midwife. The average fee was reported to be 7s.6d. On the other hand, doctors' fees ranged from 10s. to about £2. The average for an uncomplicated delivery was £1.[23] It is quite clear that a middle-class woman could afford the services of a doctor for this occasion. Even with the budget restrictions on medical expenses we have noted, there would be no problem affording several consultations during pregnancy, given the importance now attributed to childbirth.

This was an important transition for middle-class women. And far more than economics was involved. Middle-class women came to prefer the services of the doctor over those of the midwife because he had more benefits to offer. First, he had some training, more than most midwives. Second, his obstetrical instruments gave him an edge over the midwife, especially in the case of complicated deliveries. Dr. Ryan's instructions to doctors describe the doctor's advantage:

> . . . every medical obstetrician should have, in a small
> pocket case a female catheter, a tracheal pipe, a lancet,
> some morphia or opium, ergota, and a pair of scissors. He
> should also have a set of obstetrical instruments, in a leather

case consisting of a forceps, lever, blunt-hook, perforator, cranitomy forceps, crotchet, and an osteotome, which he should take with him.[24]

Also for more and more women a doctor's mere presence gave them a greater sense of security than that of the midwife.[25] Dr. Ryan's opinion was that

> . . . a midwife can afford no relief whatever and generally does harm by her interference. I never knew a woman who attended by a medical practitioner who on any future parturition would admit a midwife. I have often heard women remark how very differently they were treated by their female and their medical attendants; and that females are much more unfeeling than those of the other sex.[26]

This is quite possible because midwives were generally old women who took up midwifery because they needed the money and were not fit to do anything else.

When did the transition to doctors occur? By mid-century it was common advice for women to seek a doctor at the first signs of pregnancy and, according to Dr. Ryan, almost universal by the 1860s. He commented that 'in modern times we observe a wise and judicious preference given to male obstetricians, and midwives are scarcely ever exclusively employed unless among the ignorant or lower classes.'[27]

Thus it can be assumed with some certainty that middle-class women were using the services of a doctor with increasing frequency, at least for this very important event in her life. However, the most essential point in this discussion is the extent to which she benefited from the doctor's services. Again, one cannot assume that because there were advances in the training programs of doctors and new developments in the field of obstetrics that these advances affected the woman's health, since there was a serious lag between any advances and their benefit to the patient. At the very least, this caused her undue anxiety and needless suffering. At its worst it might result in the death of the woman. The fact that the advances in obstetrics did not significantly alter the health of the mothers' is revealed by the stability of the maternal mortality rate throughout the century. In 1838 the rate of maternal mortality was 5 to every 1000 births; in 1892 it was 4.9 to every 1000 births. More important for our purposes is that this same rough stability prevailed in the middle-class community of Camberwell also. Maternal mortality rates averaged 4 deaths per 1000 births in Camberwell as late as the 1870s and 1880s. It was only after the 1880s that Camberwell began to show a decline in its maternal mortality rates, 3.65 deaths per 1000 births.[28] Indeed one must wonder if the persistently high rate of mortality in childbirth was not a significant factor in the decision to control the number of births, a point that will be taken up in a later chapter. Admittedly, in many cases classified as accidents due to childbirth, death was unavoidable; we must not exaggerate the level of medical advance. For example, the technique of Caesarian section was not developed until the late 1870s. Effective blood transfusions were not perfected until the turn of the century.[29] Here were obvious limitations on the ability to prevent death in childbirth. It is important to note also that although overall maternal mortality rates remained relatively constant the balance between the two major causes, puerperal fever and accidents of childbirth, did change in the middle-class community of Camberwell. For most of our period the balance between the two was equal. But in the 1880s the number of deaths due to accidents of childbirth began to decline; in Camberwell the change was upwards of 40 per cent, while puerperal fever remained the same. No doubt doctors' services during delivery contributed to the decline, showing that middle-class women were ultimately wise in their choice of doctors over midwives. Also the new concern with pre-natal care contributed to the decline. But again this was belated change and it does not account for the continued high rate of mortality due to puerperal fever. Certainly, before the 1880s the effectiveness of doctors' services could easily be judged disappointing. And this was not entirely necessary; improvement in maternal health could have come about earlier. Many women suffered needlessly because of the lag between innovation and acceptance by the general medical profession.

One can point to many examples. For instance, the mother-to-be was warned over and over again how very critical the first four months of her pregnancy were, not only for her own health but also for the unborn child. She was to be most cautious during this period. Thus the well-informed woman was anxious to determine as soon as possible whether she was pregnant or not. But here the same manuals that urged great care had little to offer, for their advice identifying pregnancy was vague and traditional. Throughout the century the means of determining pregnancy remained unchanged. Women were told of the general signs: 1. 'ceasing to be unwell,' which was the euphemism for the cessation of the menses; 2. 'morning sickness,' nausea and vomiting; 3. shooting and lancinating pains and enlargement of the breast; 4. 'quickening' which was the first perception of the foetus in the womb (it was described as a fluttering of a bird in the stomach and usually occurred at a week or fortnight beyond the fourth month, or about the nineteenth week); 5. increased size after quickening. In addition, there were the accompanying signs of sleepiness, heartburn, increase flow of saliva, toothache and loss of appetite.[30] These were the only means of determining pregnancy that were made known to the Victorian woman, and moreover the woman had to wait at least five months before she was certain of her state. As Dr. Bull aptly indicated, traditional signs afforded little certainty because some of them 'are not unfrequently absent, although pregnancy did exist, and the remainder may be present, although pregnancy be absent.' He added that

Many a female, I am confident, has from this very circumstance experienced much difficulty in attaining certainty as to her state and suffered months of anxiety and doubt. This has arisen from a want of those clear notions, and that precise information, which a question so important demands.[31]

This was true when Dr. Bull first wrote his book in 1833. But soon after this, new methods of determining pregnancy earlier than five months were advanced. In 1836, J.M. Jaquemier discovered that the mucosa about the vaginal orifice and the lower portion of the anterior wall assumed a bluish discoloration in the pregnant state.[32] However, Dr. Bull never made any mention of this new sign, even in the 1877 edition. It was not until the 1880s that it first appeared in a popular manual for women. Allbutt's *The Wife's Handbook: How a Woman Should Order Herself During Pregnancy*, published in 1882, was the first to make mention that a very early and valuable sign in determining pregnancy was this discoloration of the vaginal passage. He wrote that

The skin (mucous membrane) which lines the inside of the vagina is, in a non-pregnant woman, of a rosy colour; but soon after she becomes pregnant it turns to a violet hue. With a small looking glass and a good light, a woman can with a little management, observe this change of colour herself; or better still her husband or a female neighbour could easily detect it by separating the lips and slightly distending the mouth of the vaginal passage, at the same time letting a good light shine upon the exposed parts.[33]

Another method of determining pregnancy was by examination of the size of the vagina with a vaginal speculum. The objections to the use of the vaginal speculum have already been noted. Overall, the reluctance to employ the two new methods of determining pregnancy, despite their real superiority over traditional methods, stemmed from the unwillingness to undertake an internal examination of the female patient. Only when labor was well under way would the doctor for the first time examine his patient internally.[34] The purpose of this examination, as Dr. Ryan explained in 1867, was to 'enable the obstetrician to conclude whether the woman be really in labour, whether the labour be natural or preternatural, and whether she is likely to be speedily or slowly delivered.' Dr. Ryan noted the reluctance of the patient to submit even to this exam. He advised that

the importance of the examination should be dwelt upon by

the nurse, female friend and medical practitioner, and it ought to be proposed and made as soon as possible. It is popularly termed, 'taking the pain' and by the French 'the touch,' but it can as well be made in the absence of pain.[35]

In the case of obstetrics, the reluctance of the medical profession to examine the female patient because of a sense of delicacy approached the ridiculous. Women may have contributed to the problem, as Dr. Ryan implied, but doctors had their own sensibilities. The failure to accept the vaginal speculum more readily might be understandable, but the hesitancy to apply the stethoscope to the woman's stomach to listen for the foetal heart is not. In 1816, René Théophile Hyacinthe Laennec invented the stethoscope, a landmark in medical science. In 1822, Jean Alexandre Leumeau, Vicomte de Kergaredec discovered that the instrument could detect the sound of the foetal heart. However, Kergaredec's observation was not readily accepted. James Hamilton, Professor of Midwifery at Edinburgh, rejected the idea of applying the stethoscope to the naked belly of a woman as positively indecent. Even as late as the 1860s Francis Ramsbottom, one of the foremost authorities on obstetrics in London, remained unconvinced. He stated that 'he had no personal experience of using the stethoscope for this purpose.'[36] Thus it can be seen again that a major cause for the delay in applying new knowledge and techniques to benefit the woman was due to the general conservativism of the British medical profession. Not only was it slow to accept the innovations of its colleagues, but also it sought direct action against some of the pioneers. This was the case in 1887, when Dr. Allbutt, who was noted earlier as the first to describe in an inexpensive edition a good means for early determination of pregnancy, was removed from the British Medical Register because of his publication.[37]

Given the slow advance in British medical practice, plus the fees involved, most middle-class women undoubtedly did not consult a doctor until pregnancy was well along. Indeed there was little reason to do so. But all the while they were being urged, in the manuals they bought so avidly, to take particular care in the early stages. If they listened to these urgings, which were sensible, if unspecific, recommending exercise and good diet, they may have benefited — assuming they were sure of their pregnancy. But the most obvious connection,that of early identification followed by specific advice on pre-natal care, was simply not made. Even if not beset by uncertainty, women went through most of their pregnancy on their own.

In childbirth itself, the gap between what was medically possible and what was actually offered continued. One of the most important developments in nineteenth-century obstetrics was the discovery of chloroform by James Simpson in 1847. To be sure, contrary to general opinion, there were pain killers prior to chloroform.[38] Opium was available for complicated labors. As early as 1741, Ould in his work *A Treatise on Midwifery*, urged that 'if the spirits be much exhausted and the pains grow very short and of little or no advantage than an opiate is of surpassing service.'[39] But this was not advised for normal deliveries, for opium did slow down the process of labor. This is what prompted Simpson to find a better method of alleviating pain. He was the first to apply an anaesthetic, ether, to midwifery in January of 1847. In November, Simpson tried chloroform in a labor case. It soon became the most-used anaesthesia in midwifery, and continued as such for the next century. It was quicker to act than ether, more portable, free from fire hazards and could be administered without any elaborate apparatus. And it allowed the process of labor to continue naturally while the pains usually attendant upon it were altogether abrogated.[40] The controversy which developed over the general employment of chloroform in labor cases was most dramatic because, in this instance, there was no reluctance to the innovation on the part of the woman. The voice of objection and caution came, in large part, from other doctors.

What was the Victorian woman's reaction to Simpson's discovery? The story is told that the first woman to be administered chloroform in childbirth was so delighted at her freedom from pain that she christened the baby girl Anaesthesia.[41] This illustrates the general feeling. In 100 cases in which chloroform was used in delivery, Dr. Simpson reported that

> I do not remember a single patient to have taken it who has not afterwards declared her sincere gratification for its employment, and her indubitable determination to have recourse again to similar means under similar circumstances. Most indeed, have subsequently set out, like zealous missionaries, to persuade other friends to avail themselves of the same measure of relief in their hour of trial and travail.[42]

In his article, *An Account of a New Anaesthetic Agent, as a Substitute for Sulphuric Ether in Surgery and Midwifery*, he correctly observed that 'obstetricians may oppose it, but I believe our patients themselves will force the use of it upon the profession.'[43] Here indeed was a means of developing the kind of greater control over the natural process of childbirth that middle-class women were obviously seeking.

Nevertheless, the debate over the use of chloroform continued for many years in the British medical journals. Contrary to popular opinion it did not die away with the administering of chloroform to Queen Victoria in 1857 with the birth of her last child.[44] In 1862 Dr. Charles Kidd in an article in *The London Medical Review* was still defending the safety of chloroform in obstetrical cases. He reported that 'as to the safety of chloroform in obstetric practice, it may be said that in about 30,000 obstetric cases of various kinds up to the year 1860, there was not a single fatal accident correctly ascribed to chloroform.'[45] It was not until the 1877 edition of Dr. Bull's best seller, *Hints to Mothers,* that the benefits of chloroform were recognized – another example of the British medical profession's slow adaptation to change. Here was an opportunity to allay the woman's fear of the pains of childbirth and to help her through her delivery, but many doctors failed to take advantage of it for several decades.[46]

The most serious and tragic result of delay in the application of advances in medical knowledge concerned puerperal fever. Even if a woman was fortunate enough to have an uncomplicated and easy delivery she still had to face the most critical stage of childbirth, for it was after the baby was born the mother was most likely to die. And all the care she took to manage herself properly as advised in her manuals could not in most cases have helped. The victim of puerperal fever could not prepare herself against it. The horror of women dying in childbirth due to this cause was most piercing in the nineteenth century, and in the middle class perhaps above all, because many of the deaths could and should have been avoided.

Puerperal fever was the single most common cause of death in childbirth in the nineteenth century. It was a septic poisoning. Puerperal fever, or Metria as it was sometimes referred to, began a few hours to a few days after the birth of the child. There was a high fever and all the symptoms accompanying what is still called 'blood-poisoning.'[47] The tragedy lies in the fact that even by the end of the eighteenth century, all the knowledge that was needed to prevent puerperal fever had been acquired. A brief outline of the medical advances made concerning puerperal fever will prove the point.

In the late seventeenth century, William Harvey recognized the significance of the large internal wound following separation of the placenta as the starting point of the infection, and advised intra-uterine injections. In 1773, Charles White, in his work, *A Treatise on the Management of Pregnant and Lying-In Women*, stressed the importance of fresh air, cleanliness and postural change. He wrote that

> As soon as the woman is delivered as it can conveniently be done, clean linen should be put about her . . . In a few hours after delivery, as soon as the patient has had a little rest, she should sit up in bed . . . This frequent upright position is of the utmost consequence, and cannot be too much enforced. It prevents the lochia from stagnating, the stools and urine from being too long retained, and promotes the contraction of the uterus. The chamber door, and even the windows, if the weather be warm should be opened

every day.[48]

In 1975, Alexander Gordon found the most important key to the problem when he discovered the mode of spread of the dread disease. In his work *A Treatise on the Epidemic Puerperal Fever of Aberdeen*, he made the most important observation that 'this disease seized such women only as were visited, or delivered by a practitioner or taken care of by a nurse, who had previously attended patients affected with the disease.'[49] Thus he insisted that all midwives and doctors carefully wash themselves and change their clothing before attending a pregnant woman. Although the practical cause remained to be discovered, there would have been few epidemics of puerperal fever in the nineteenth century if these prophylactic measures had been generally adopted. Unfortunately, doctors failed regularly to wash their hands or even change their clothing, for they were busy men and medical school advice was easily ignored. And here was the real irony, for the middle-class conversion to a doctor's care could actually heighten the role of puerperal fever.

In the nineteenth century Ignaz Semmelweis, the Hungarian obstetrician who practised in Vienna, made a valuable contribution to the fight against puerperal fever. The story of his realization of the cause of the much higher death rate in the wards run by his medical students than those by midwives is an important part of medical history. Semmelweis made the same demand that Gordon did in 1795. His instructions were that all who came into the lying-in wards had first to scrub with chloride of lime before touching any patient. Semmelweis's discoveries were brought to London by E.H.F. Routh, although only in 1848. In a paper read before the Royal Medical and Chirurgical Society, he reported on Semmelweis' work and strongly urged the adoption of his practice. The paper caused much discussion and while many present agreed that there was a risk of infection, there was no unanimity about the best way to check it.[50] Hence, many thousands of Victorian women continued to suffer and die, when a simple remedy was literally at the medical profession's fingertips. Graph 4 shows the number of women who died annually from puerperal fever from 1847-77. It can be seen that epidemics raged as late as 1872 and that there was no tendency toward *per capita* decline.[51]

A probably disproportionate percentage of the women who died from puerperal fever were middle-class. In Camberwell the number of women dying from puerperal fever remained constant throughout our period and later. The number of deaths averaged 2 per 1000 which was comparable to London's rate but higher than England's rate as a whole, which was 1.9.[52] It must be remembered that puerperal fever was not a result of poverty, overcrowding or lack of nutrition. Lower-class women undoubtedly could encounter the strep poisoning which caused the fever through diseases of the other members of their family or the

87

Graph 4 Number of Annual Deaths Attributed to Puerperal Fever in England, 1847-1877

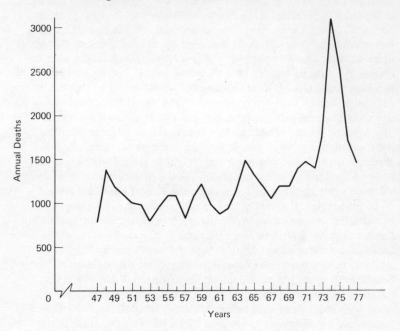

Source: Registrar General's Report for the Years 1847-77.

uncleanliness of the midwives who attended them. It seems quite probable that conversion from midwife to doctor may have heightened the risk for many middle-class women, particularly if we assume that the midwives previously employed by the middle-class, the better-paid group, were likely to have some sense of personal cleanliness. Certainly widespread conversion to doctors had no impact on the *per capita* incidence of puerperal fever through the 1890s. The simple fact was, as Semmelweis' data suggested, that a doctor came into contact with a wider variety of infectious diseases in his practice than did a midwife. Whereas the midwife's practice was confined to maternity cases, the doctor brought to his patient new hazards. He could and did carry to the parturient woman laudable pus from his surgical cases, droplets from scarlet fever cases and putrefaction from the corpses he dissected. The irony of the situation is dramatic. The middle-class woman sought the services of the doctor in order to provide the best measures for her own health and that of the child, and by doing so, she left herself a victim to the largest cause of maternal mortality, puerperal fever.

Thus it can be seen that the woman's anxieties about her condition were realistic. Her fears about the pains of childbirth and possible death were not greatly alleviated in the nineteenth century, although they could have been had the British medical profession not been so slow to recognize the real needs of women. This reluctance to change owed much to a general traditionalism but it also reflected the medical profession's prejudices about women. The general consensus of opinion by doctors was that women were by nature emotional beings, subject to nervous disorders. This in turn prompted an overemphasis on the emotional aspects of a woman's life, when in reality there should have been more concentration on her physical state. The downgrading of physical changes and the stress on emotional aspects colored discussions of the management of pregnancy. Ignorance accounts for part of this. Unable to explain the physical phenomena, doctors argued them away with references to the 'typical' emotional behavioral problems of women. And the doctors were not shy in informing the general public of the primacy of the emotions. Dr. Conquest stressed that

> . . . there is another aspect of most material consequence to
> the health of the female . . . I mean the due regulation of
> her mental constitution, and her moral feelings and
> affections. . . To what use is it carefully to observe the
> external and physical laws of health, if in herself she raises
> an agent more powerful to subvert her health than they are
> to preserve it? The influence of strong or violent mental
> emotion, whether exciting — as of joy, hope, anger, or rage;
> or depressing — as of fear and despair, we well know to
> surpress a powerful and immediate influence over the vital

functions. Death has often followed instantaneously. . .[53]
A woman's emotions were not only responsible for her disabilities but
also affected the child's health. It was contended seriously that

> A child born of a mother, long time depressed by sorrow or
> agitated by contending or ungovernable emotions is seldom
> natural, seldom sound in its organization; too often is its
> constitution, thus enfeebled and predisposed, rendered a
> ready prey to the cause of physical and mental disease.[54]

Another example of the prejudices against women and their
health problems was found in the discussion about the pains of
delivery. It was implied by some doctors that middle-class women
suffered pain during childbirth because they led very unnatural lives.[55]
Soft living was the cause of difficulty in delivery, it was argued; there
was no problem with delivery of working-class women. It was pointed
out that it was very common in England for servant girls who became
illegitimately pregnant, to absent themselves for an hour or two and, after
giving birth to a child, to return to the discharge of their household
duties.[56] Here, doctors echoed the moralism so common in judging
middle-class life.

Obviously some of the reluctance to apply chloroform to the women
in labor followed from this general opinion doctors held of middle-class
women. To some extent the doctors may have created a self-fulfilling
prophecy. Great anxiety and insecurity were part of the process of
childbirth. Despite the important transition from midwife to doctor,
the physical aspects of childbirth remained little changed during the
course of the nineteenth century. And all the while doctors and manuals
on motherhood warned of responsibilities while suggesting that women
by their nature might be unfit to shoulder them and that middle-class
women were, at least in terms of their physical constitution, less fit than
others. Small wonder that middle-class women who were seeking modest
improvements in comfort and other aspects of their lives, feared the
process of childbirth. And their problems did not end with a safe
delivery. The birth of the child brought them new anxieties, which, as
usual, the manuals they consulted were quick to emphasize.

Notes

1. Banks and Banks, *Feminism*, pp. 61-3.
2. Ansell, *On the Rate of Mortality*, p. 59.
3. Warren, *My House on Two Hundred Pounds*, p. 34.
4. Tilt, *Elements of Health*, p. 268.
5. Henry Allbutt, 'Evil Produced by Over-Bearing, and Excessive Lactation,' *Malthusian Tract No. 4* (1880s?) p. 2.
6. Ansell, *On the Rate of Mortality*, p. 49

7. Ibid. p. 46.
8. In the second half of the century, middle-class women would be practising birth control and this would limit some aspects of her problem as mother (a full discussion of birth control is found in Chapter 6).
9. *The Magazine of Domestic Economy*, Vol. II (March 1844), p. 391.
10. Dr. Thomas Bull, *Hints to Mothers, for the Management of Health during the Period of Pregnancy and Lying-In Room; with an Exposure of Popular Errors in Connection with Those Subjects* (London, 1837).
11. Dr. John T. Conquest, *Letters to a Mother on the Management of Herself and Her Children in Health and Disease: Embracing the Subjects of Pregnancy, Childbirth, Nursing, Food, Exercise, Bathing, Clothing, Etc., Etc.: With Remarks on Chloroform* (London, 1848).
12. Henry A. Allbutt, *The Wife's Handbook: How A Woman Should Order Herself During Pregnancy, in the Lying-In Room, and After Delivery, With Hints on the Management of the Baby and Other Matters of Importance Necessary to be known by a Married Woman* (London, 1886); *Every Mother's Handbook: A Guide to the Management of Her Children from Birth Through Infancy and Childhood with Instructions for Preliminary Treatment of Accidents and Illness* (London, 1897).
13. *The Mother's Friend: A Monthly Magazine* (London, 1848-95).
14. F. Poynter (ed.), *The Evolution of Medical Practice in Britain* (London, 1961), p. 63.
15. Walter Radcliffe, *Milestones in Midwifery* (Bristol, 1967), p. 95.
16. Graham, *Eternal Eve*, p. 146.
17. Ibid, p. 147.
18. *Fifth Annual Report of The Registrar General of Births, Deaths and Marriages in England* (London, 1843), pp. 380-81.
19. Radcliffe, *Milestones in Midwifery*, p. 95.
20. *The British Medical Journal* (3 April 1875).
21. *Report from the Select Committee on Midwives Registration*, Vol. X.2. (June 1892), *passim.*
22. *Census of England and Wales*, 1891.
23. *Select Committee on Midwives Registration*, p. 149.
24. Dr. Michael Ryan, *The Philosophy of Marriage, in its Social, Moral, and Physical Relations: With An Account of the Diseases of the Genita-Urinary Organs which Impair or Destroy the Reproductive Function and Induce a Variety of Complaints, with the Physiology of Generations in the Vegetable and Animal Kingdom, Being Part of a Course of Obstetric Lectures Delivered at the North London School of Medicine* (London, 1837), pp. 210-11.
25. Conquest, *Letters to a Mother*, p. 39; *The Mother's Home-Book; a Book for Her Own and Her Children's Management with Hints and Helps for Every-Day Emergencies* (London, 1879), p. 13.
26. Ryan, *The Philosophy of Marriage*, p. 202.
27. Ibid., p. 209.
28. The above figures are recorded in the following combination of volumes of the *Annual Report of the Registrar General*; Vol. XVII (1884-85), pp. lxxii 1, 2, 63; Vol. XXIII-I (1895), p. 193.
29. Radcliffe, *Milestones in Midwifery*, pp. 95-9.
30. Pye Henry Charasse, *Advice to a Wife on the Management of her own Health*, (London, 1842), pp. 66-7.
31. Bull, *Hints to Mothers*, p. 27.
32. Ricci, *One Hundred Years*, p. 23.
33. Allbutt, *The Wife's Handbook*, p. 21.
34. Radcliffe, *Milestones in Midwifery*, p. 97.

35. Ryan, *The Philosophy of Marriage*, p. 212.
36. Radcliffe, *Milestones in Midwifery*, pp. 71-2.
37. Glass, "Population and Population Movements," *Population Policies*, p. 35.
38. Burton, *The Pageant of Early Victorian England*, pp. 172-3.
39. Graham, *Eternal Eve*, p. 165.
40. Radcliffe, *Milestones in Midwifery*, p. 81.
41. Graham, *Eternal Eve*, p. 263; Burton, *The Pageant of Early Victorian England*, p. 176.
42. Quoted from Conquest's *Letters to a Mother*, p. 13.
43. James Y. Simpson, *An Account of a New Anaesthetic Agent, as a Substitute for Sulphuric Ether in Surgery and Midwifery* (1848), quoted in Radcliffe, *Milestones in Midwifery*, p. 84.
44. Burton, *The Pageant of Early Victorian England*, p. 177.
45. Charles Kidd, "On Chloroform and Some of its Clinical Uses," *The London Medical Review or Monthly Journal of Medical and Surgical Science*, Vol. II (July 1861-June 1862), p. 244.
46. The following argument may strike the twentieth-century observer as excessively speculative, for we now know that some of the warnings against excessive uses of chloroform were correct. But twentieth-century medical knowledge cannot in this case and others be used neatly to explain nineteenth-century conservatism. This general problem is discussed in the chapter appendix, with regard to anaesthetics and other examples of nineteenth-century medical practices concerning women.
47. Graham, *Eternal Eve*, p. 193.
48. Dr. Charles White, *A Treatise on the Management of Pregnant and Lying-In Women* (1773), quoted in Radcliffe, *Milestones in Midwifery*, p. 66.
49. Dr. Alexander Gordon, *A Treatise of the Epidemic Puerperal Fever of Aberdeen* (1795), quoted in Radcliffe, *Milestones in Midwifery*, p. 65.
50. Ibid., p. 51.
51. *Seventeenth Annual Report of the Registrar General of Births, Deaths and Marriages in England*, p. 84.
52. *Annual Report of the Registrar General of Births, Deaths and Marriages in England,* Vol. XVII (1884-85), pp. lxii, 3, 63, 162-73; Vol. XXIII-1 (1895), p. 123.
53. Conquest, *Letters to a Mother*, p. 11.
54. Ibid., p. 12.
55. Ibid., pp. 1-2; Ryan, *The Philosophy of Marriage*, p. 209.
56. Conquest, *Letters to a Mother*, p. 48.

APPENDIX I, CHAPTER 4

The preceding chapter has established three dramatic examples of gaps between available techniques and treatment which were particularly tragic for nineteenth-century middle-class women. It is of course essential for a social historian dealing with medicine to consult contemporary medical authorities for possible explanations of earlier health developments. A doctor seeking to defend his profession could offer something of an excuse for the failure to conduct internal examinations early in pregnancy during the nineteenth century. These examinations could not in fact provide positive proof of pregnancy. Nevertheless early examinations remained desirable to provide the doctor and patient with knowledge of the date of conception, particularly in cases where an induced birth might be necessary. Early examination was also vital, as French doctors noted in the 1840s, to predict possible complications. Finally, only an internal exam could determine whether cessation of the menses had been caused by a cystic ovary or some other disorder. Thus the failure to utilize available methods remained a serious omission.

With regard to chloroform the present-day physician can properly note danger of death from overdose and damage to the liver from prolonged use. Yet these factors barely apply to the nineteenth-century practice. It was true that a few physicians warned of possible death but their reasoning derived from a reluctance to interfere with the natural process and not from any careful testing of the actual use of chloroform. As it was, the pioneers in the use of anaesthesia could produce clear figures on the virtually absence of death due to overdose in delivery. No one advocated or employed excessive amounts of chloroform during delivery; even a small dosage was intended for the last, painful stages of delivery alone. The opponents of the use of chloroform in the nineteenth century were not objecting to chloroform *per se*, but to all anaesthesia. They were reacting with a conservative unwillingness to innovate and lacked physiological evidence to support their position.

Finally the incidence of puerperal fever among the middle class cannot be explained away at all. Some twentieth-century doctors point to an increase in strep infections, notably scarlet fever, lasting into the 1920s; the implication of this argument is that the women themselves brought the infection into the delivery room, and that doctors' blunders had nothing to do with the problem. That strep infection may have contributed to a dramatic upsurge in puerperal fever such as that of the late seventies is possible and worthy of further investigation. But it cannot serve as a sufficient explanation. Puerperal fever rates in

France did not oscillate in the same pattern as in England and yet scarlet fever epidemics were Europe-wide. France faced her crisis of puerperal fever towards the end of the century as more of the population began to employ doctors.[1] More important, the high incidence of puerperal fever rates in Camberwell simply cannot relate to any explanation relying on epidemics of strep, because Camberwell was not the seat of some peculiarly localized outbreak of scarlet fever. The fact was that the doctor's own practices formed a vital part of the explanation of high incidence of puerperal fever among the middle class and for the persistence of the disease into the twentieth century. This was noted specifically by Louis Pasteur who, after listening to a variety of exculpations offered by his colleagues in 1879, showed dramatically that the problem was in the doctor's failure to wash or change clothing.[2] Discussion of the subject in England revealed similarly that most doctors were blithely unconvinced of this same necessity. Thus while present-day medical opinion may elaborate the explanation for the gap between knowledge and practice, the gap remains.

Notes

1. *Statistique de la France, Mouvement de la population*, 1858 ff.
2. Paul Bar, 'Leçon inaugurale,' in Pierre Budin, *La Chaire de clinique obstetricale à la Faculté de medicine de Paris* (Paris, 1908).

6 A NEW MODEL OF CHILD CARE

The Victorian woman's life would never be quite the same with the birth of her first child. Most of her thoughts, her worries, and her energies would revolve around her child, and with each child the responsibilities grew more and more intense. She did not feel confident in the adequacy of her maternal instincts and so she worried continually about her child and its care. Her major concern was for the child's health. With every sickness of childhood, the mother's anxieties heightened. Even the most basic aspects of child care, for example, feeding and discipline, were to create serious problems for her. She continually sought advice on the best method of care for her child. But in the end, as was the case with her own health, there was very little she could do to improve the child's situation given the limited means available and the traditionalism which still maintained a strong hold on this part of her life.

With each new birth, the Victorian mother experienced many anxious moments wondering if the babe would live or die. The fate of thousands of infants dying prematurely every year was to become a burning issue in Victorian society. The outcry against the needless tragedy of infant mortality continued throughout the century. The sentiment expressed was similar to that concerning the state of maternal mortality, but more intense because of the greater numbers involved and the helplessness of the victim. A declining sense of fatalism and a growing determination that this tragedy need not be, were again much in evidence. A typical reaction was that of Dr. Alfred Fennings, author of *Every Mother's Book: or the Child's Best Doctor*, who noted that

> The OMNISCIENT GOD never intended that nearly half the babies born in this country should die as they now do, before they are five years old. Carelessness . . . and a general ignorance of simple and safe remedies to cure their peculiar diseases have been the fatal causes.[1]

Dr. R. Hall Bakewell, who wrote a series of articles on 'Infant Mortality, and Its Causes' for *The British Mothers' Journal*, was of the same belief.

> We cannot deny that there must be something wrong in the management of children during the early years. Children are not sent into the world to die, they are sent to live to a natural term of man's life; and a system by which one-fifth of all who are born never see the first anniversary of their birth, must be radically wrong somewhere.[2]

These are just two examples of the growing concern over infant care. There were hundreds of books published and articles written specifically on child care. The books were widely publicized: for example, Dr. Fennings' book was advertised regularly in *The Mothers' Friend*, a monthly magazine. One of the advertisements made the following claim:

> Do not let your children die. Fennings' *Every Mother's Book* contains everything a mother ought to know about her child's Feeding, Teething, Sleeping, Weaning, also Hints, Cautions, Remedies for all diseases, and Secrets worth 500 Guineas. Mothers and Fathers, save your child's life by reading it. Its instructions have already saved thousands.[3]

However, in spite of the intense concern, in spite of the sage advice, infant mortality remained a perplexing problem for the Victorian mother. The infant deathbed scene so popular with the religious writers, the grief of a bereaved mother at the loss of her child, which was a regular feature in many of the women's magazines, reflected grim reality. The annual reports of the Registrar General for England and Wales indicated that for the period 1839-51, the annual number of deaths of infants under one was between 150-160 per 1000 births.[4] In the late forties, infant mortality was even greater than this general average. The Registrar General reported 88,784 deaths of children under one out of 539,965 births, approximately 164 deaths in 1000 births.[5] It was to decline but only slightly, as Graph 5 indicates, during the rest of the century. For a brief few years, 1876-90, there was a steady drop, but in the nineties the rate soared again. By 1899, it was close to the 1847 record, 163 deaths in 1000 births. About 20 per cent of all deaths annually struck children less than one year old.

These persistently high rates of infant mortality are indeed disturbing in view of the assumed improvements in sanitation, living conditions and medicine. Why did infant mortality not decline consistently in the nineteenth century? There is no simple explanation, but many of the reasons relate to those noted on the section on women's health, as will be shown later.

Childhood mortality, that is deaths among children aged one to five, did improve slightly as indicated in Graph 6. Even these rates remained higher than might be assumed from a general knowledge of nineteenth-century progress, and their decline was too slow to fulfill the Victorian woman's own expectations, as illustrated by the following lament:

> It is a known fact that forty per cent, or nearly one-half of all deaths in the United Kingdom, are those of children under five years of age, while nearly one-fifth of all children die within twelve months of their birth. Now this is a disgrace to such a civilized country as ours . . .[6]

The Victorian woman expected child mortality to decrease. The persistence of a high rate profoundly sharpened the mother's concern for her child, making the fear of death very real.

Graph 5   Deaths of Children Under One Year, 1861-1900

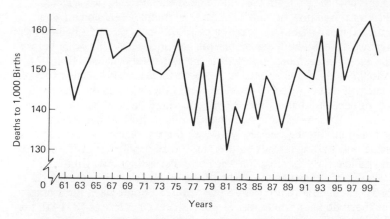

Source: Helem M. Cobbold, *Statistical Analysis of Infant Mortality, and its causes in the United Kingdom,* (London, 1910), Table I.

Graph 6   Annual Death Rate From 0-5 years 1841-1890

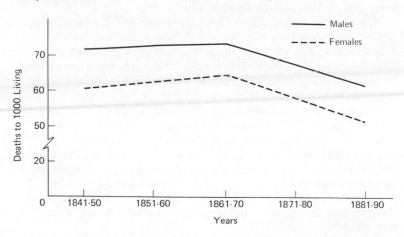

Source: *Annual Registrar General's Reports,* 1841-1890

It is legitimate to cite the national rates of child mortality because in this case the problem the middle class encountered was scarcely different. We know of individual cases of middle-class women who suffered greatly from the loss of a child; for example, Mrs. Beeton lost her two first children, one before the age of one, and the other before the age of three. More important is the statistical evidence. Even Ansell's study of the upper and professional classes in the year 1874 indicated that close to 10 per cent of all infants would die before the age of one, and that another 3 per cent would be dead before the age of five.[7] These rates were significantly under those of the general population. But they suggest that even the top segment of society had made only halting inroads on this traditional problem. For the bulk of the middle class the situation was more distressing. Data from Camberwell dramatize the plight of the middle class. For the period 1851-61 child mortality was 26 per cent, at a point when the average for the nation as a whole was 21 per cent. Even as late as 1871-80, the Camberwell rate of child mortality remained as high as the nation's average, at 24 per cent. In other words all the diligent efforts of the middle-class mother made little impact either in comparison to society as a whole or over time. Camberwell did have a slight edge over London, whose infant mortality for the years 1871-80 averaged 15.8 per cent compared to Camberwell's 14.7 per cent; overall child mortality was 27 per cent to 24 per cent respectively.[8] It is important to note that Camberwell was able to improve its child mortality rates more than its infant mortality rates in comparison to that of a general urban population. Here was where the new levels of maternal care might pay off. But in this period the gains were only slight and the emotional investment in the child remained extremely risky.

A look as the causes of death among children will show the problems that faced the Victorian mother. Among the diseases most fatal to young children in the nineteenth century were pneumonia, convulsions, measles, scarlet fever, whooping cough, smallpox, diarrhea, teething, and atrophy (lack of nutrition). Almost regardless of class, there was little help to be found from the medical profession in dealing with infant illness, especially for the epidemic diseases such as scarlet fever and measles. Pediatric care was non-existent in the nineteenth century, for the medical profession showed very little interest in children's diseases; there were not even the theoretical and technological advances that occurred in obstetrics and gynecology, the one exception being the smallpox vaccination. For the middle-class mother who found it increasingly difficult to accept infant death, this meant a fearsome increase in her responsibilities — for there was no one to care for the sick child.

Of course, one must hope for more precise statistics on the actual incidence of the mortal diseases among middle-class children. Lower-class children, lacking proper nourishment, clothing and housing, were certainly more likely to succumb to the communicable disease. But, if only to a lesser degree, middle-class families faced some of the same problems. There is certainly ample evidence that the middle-class mother was made acutely conscious of the danger of disease and death.

In fact, the middle-class mother was held largely responsible for the continuing high rate of mortality. According to most of the authorities on the subject of infant care, the mother's mis-management of the child was largely to blame for the thousands of unfortunate deaths. At times the criticism of the woman implied infanticide on her part. The following statement from *The British Mothers' Journal* was typical of the harshness of the accusations made against the mother. It held that

There is something very wrong somewhere, for so far from living to growing old, forty babies out of every hundred born in this country, die before they have lived 5 years. Why do these things happen? Who does them? Ah, 'thereby hangs a tale,' a strange and sad one, which we women would do well to listen to. On our shoulders lies the greater part of the blame — *we* fill the churchyards, and send babies a short cut from the cradle to the grave — we kill them by our bad management. Almost every baby comes into the world quite strong and healthy enough to live long and to have good health; it is *we* who cut life short, just as truly as we cut off tape with our scissors; it is *we* who too often *make* illness, just as truly as we make puddings or pinafores. Yes, women have been in the world six thousand years, and still up to this very day we do not know how to manage our little ones. Then it is surely high time we begin to learn for the churchyards are quite full enough.[9]

Dr. Bakewell concurred with the above opinion. He wrote that

It must be clear that these are errors in the physical education of infants — errors in the habits of mothers, which are as wide-spread and deeply rooted as families themselves.[10]

This type of criticism of the mother continued throughout the period. Whether or not it is true remains to be seen, but the very fact that these harsh accusations were made repeatedly must have affected the woman's sense of security in managing her own child. As in so many other aspects of her life, the woman sought new advice and received devastating criticism.

One of the first problems the woman faced in caring for her child was feeding. It was reported that one of the most frequent causes of yearly deaths of young children was improper feeding, the result often being atrophy or diarrhea.[11] In the nineteenth century, the middle-class woman had three methods of feeding her child: breast-feeding the child herself, hiring a wet-nurse, or artificial feeding, which was sometimes referred to as 'bringing-up by hand.' All the authorities on infant management agreed that the one and only proper source of nourishment for the child was the mother's breast. Even though this was the most natural process, according to the authorities, it seems from the length of the discussion on the subject that more and more women needed to be reminded of this fact. The emphasis in these discussions was on the benefits of nursing for the mother rather than the baby. Dr. Conquest's remarks on the positive aspects of nursing were quite typical. He tried to impress upon the woman the following marvels found in nursing:

> This operation independent of the pleasant sensations it communicates, kindles her best affections, sweetens her most anxious cares, and in the result which it achieves for her, is an ample compensation for the privation, temporary and slender, which she may be compelled to submit to. And as a further inducement, it should be remembered that medical men concur in their opinion, that very rarely does a constitution suffer from suckling; whilst the health of many women is most materially improved by the performance of the duties of a nurse. Delicate females are generally strengthened by nursing, and many complaints incident to women are removed by it . . . fewer women die whilst nursing than at any other period of life; and it is a very common observation that their spirits are more lively and uniform, their tempers milder and more equitable, and their general feelings more healthy and pleasant, than under any other circumstance. Moreover, it is a matter of universal observation and acknowledgement that at no period is the countenance of the female more attractive, the expression more soft and beautiful, or the colour of the skin more delicate.[12]

Dr. Allbutt also went into a long discussion on the benefits of nursing for the mother. He added that women who nurse seldom miscarried, and that nervousness and hysteria were often cured by suckling.[13] Another important asset of nursing often noted was that it prevented conception. Dr. Conquest added to his already long list of benefits the following:

> . . . a woman who suckles her children, has generally an interval of a year and a half, or two years, between each confinement, but she, who, without an adequate cause for the omission, does not nurse, must expect to bear a child every twelve months, and must reconcile her mind to a shattered constitution and early old age.[14]

100

Dr. Tilt urged nursing the child in order to prevent pregnancy. His remark was that

> ... nursing, generally speaking, prevents conception up to
> 10 months, so it prevents the ruin of the mother's
> constitution by the too rapid bringing forth of children and
> we might even add, prevents a deterioration of the race, by
> the imperfect bringing-up of this too-fast-got family.[15]

At the very least these long discussions suggest that many middle-class women needed persistent encouragement to nurse their children. And indeed an increasing number chose not to; the fact was observed by their contemporaries. The reasons for the new decision on the part of middle-class women are complex. And it is again necessary to sort out myth from reality.

It is generally assumed that the middle-class mother had little time to spend with her child and left it to be cared for by a wet-nurse.[16] This image is again due in part to the Victorian woman's contemporary critics; for example, Dr. Lionel Weatherly, author of *The Young Wife's Own Book*, remarked that

> Fashion has lately stepped in among a certain class of women
> in an iniquitous manner, in her curious and inscrutable way,
> and has attempted to prevent this true mother's mission
> from being accomplished; and largely mothers are glad for
> the sake of getting rid of them.[17]

How many middle-class women employed wet-nurses in the nineteenth century? No clear statistical evidence on the number of wet-nurses is available at any point during the century. This is due to the problem noted earlier, of nurses not being classified into specialities. According to one recent study, wet-nurses disappeared in this period. This opinion is based on the decreasing number of advertisements carried for wet-nurses in the papers. It was noted that in 1822, *The Times* carried an advertisement for a wet-nurse once every four days; in 1873, one every six days; in 1882 once every twelve days, and from then on wet-nurses were neither asked for nor offered themselves.[18] Obviously, this is far from conclusive evidence.

However, it seems very probable that middle-class women resorted to wet-nurses less and less. One very important reason the difficulty of affording or even finding a suitable nurse, especially if a mother followed the recommendations for a wet-nurse as set by the manuals. Dr. Tilt urged that the wet-nurse come from the country 'not only because the circumstances of a country life are more conducive to health, but because in a small place, everything is known about everybody, and it is therefore easier to obtain a nurse whose antecedents of health and morals are known to have been good.' He recommended that her hair be brown and dark rather than flaxen or red because, in the latter, the milk was less rich in nutrient value and she was more liable to inflammation of the breast.[19] The restrictiveness of the qualifications for a wet-nurse can be seen in the guidelines set forth by *The Mother's Medical Adviser*. It stated that

> Her breath should be sweet, and perspiration free from smell; her gums firm and of good colour; teeth fine, white and perfect; she should have an abundance of milk, should have been confined about the same time as the mother of the child to be suckled; her breasts should be of a moderate size, the veins plump, the nipple conical, brown and well proportioned, neither large nor small. Her milk should be white, inodorous, inclining to a sweet taste neither watery or thick, of moderate consistence, separating into courd over a slow fire. The age of the nurse should be from 20-35; she should be mild and sprightly, good tempered and watchful.[20]

How many brown-haired country girls aged 20-35, having a child the same age as the mother's, and possessing perfect teeth, perfect skin, well-proportioned breasts, good breath and pleasant disposition were available?

The growing criticism of the wet-nurse in the literature of the day would also deter women from using a wet-nurse; for example, an article in *The British Mother's Journal* insisted that all wet-nurses were illegitimate mothers who made a living out of this evil system in society.[21] Some of the arguments against wet-nurses were based on traditional beliefs. Mothers were warned that even if the nurse was in perfect health, they could never be sure if the nurse had mental and moral afflictions, which the babe would imbibe from the nurse. It was still believed that breast milk was magic[21] and with it the baby took on something both of the physical appearance and moral character of the nurse. Most of the arguments reflected the middle class's growing concern for the child. The main contention was that the wet-nurse could never extend the same meticulous care and interest as the mother, with the result that she was careless and this often led to tragedy. It was claimed that out of 1000 infants nursed by the mother, about 300 died, but of the same number nursed out 500 died.[22]

A new attitude toward child-bearing, which will be discussed more fully later in the chapter, increasingly inhibited the mother from hiring a stranger to suckle her child. Nineteenth-century child-bearing was evolving toward increasingly intimate and loving bonds between the mother and child. Since in the English situation, the wet-nurse resided in the home, the pangs of jealousy and anxieties of a mother when she saw the affections of her child transferred to a hireling would certainly have made many middle-class mothers reluctant to give their child over to a wet-nurse. In fact, it seems fairly clear that middle-class mothers did not resort to wet-nurses extensively at any point during the nineteenth century, despite the pattern that has long been assumed. The considerable discussion of wet-nurses as the only alternative to nursing in the manuals was almost completely irrelevant to the middle-class situation, in this as in so many respects. The actual change in feeding patterns occurred not with the decline of wet nursing but with the rise of artificial feeding – and here the middle-class woman acted in direct opposition to the advice the manuals offered.

The improvement in artificial feedings developed in the second half of the century made this alternative quite attractive to the middle-class mother. An article in the *Englishwoman's Domestic Magazine* on 'A New Food for Infants,' which appeared in 1869, reflected a changing attitude. It stated that

Bread and Milk Flour is the name of the new compound designed for babies food – prepared in a few minutes with water only. When we consider that in addition to the natural grief of mothers who are denied the privilege of nursing their infants, they are in many cases compelled to submit to the worry, annoyance, and expense of maintaining a wet-nurse, we heartily welcome a substitution for the great desideratum the mother's milk.[23]

When objections to cow's milk were finally overcome aided by the development of pasteurization and its nutrient values recognized, the attractiveness of bottle feeding was greatly enhanced. The ever-increasing number of bottles and nipples being produced, as was noted in Bull's 1877 edition to *Hints to Mothers*,[24] indicates that there must have been a growing demand for these items. It should also be noted that the objections to artificial feeding were not based so much on bottle feeding, as on spoon feeding, which prior to the glass bottle was the usual method, referred to as 'bringing-up by hand.'

From the viewpoint of the Victorian mother, it seems quite evident that she did not find nursing as natural, desirable and beneficial to her as was claimed. If she did there would have been no need for the long discussions on the benefits of nursing and would never have been the growing demand for better methods of artificial feeding. The problems endured by the mother while nursing were generally put aside by observers as merely temporary discomforts. But this was not the feeling of many Victorian women; for example, even Mrs. Beeton observed that 'Lactation is always an exhausting process . . . The nine or twelve months a woman usually suckles must be, to some extent, to most mothers a period of privation and penance'.[25] The mother who suffered from milk fever, engorged breasts, cracked nipples, and general fatigue did not view these discomforts so lightly, yet these were all very common ailments that many women endured with nursing. For with every discussion of the joys of nursing, there was always a section on remedies for its many problems. A common suggestion for milk fever was that

> The breasts must be first gently emptied of their content,
> by drawing off all the milk they contain, by a breast pump,
> a nipple glass or by the mouth. The mouth of a blind puppy
> when one can be obtained, is of all means the best that can
> be employed for this purpose.[26]

Certainly a mother who had a full household and other small children to take care of found these discomforts quite distressing, and the bottle to be a blessing. This is one more example of the Victorian woman's desire to gain control of her personal comfort, the same impulse that caused the growing interest in chloroform during labor. In both cases women moved toward alleviation of suffering without real encouragement from doctors or manuals of advice. Clearly, Victorian women increasingly decided that pain and discomfort were neither acceptable nor, to the extent that traditionalists still maintained, necessary.

However, the problems with feeding did not end with the questions of method. A constant source of worry for the mother was whether or not the child was getting sufficient food. No doubt this worry was heightened by the annual reports of the Registrar General, whose conclusions were picked up by middle-class magazines, which attributed thousands of deaths yearly to a lack of nutrition. In her real anxiety about her child's health, the middle-class mother might overfeed her child, causing it serious harm and often death. This overfeeding could be related to the fact that many mothers new to the middle class found that they had ample food, and through their good intentions to give the child a special advantage simply went to excess. Here new affection for the child could prove counter-productive. Overfeeding was a problem often discussed in the manuals; for example, Mrs. Beeton observed that

> One of the most common errors that mothers fall into while
> suckling their children, is that of fancying they are always
> hungry, and consequently overfeeding them; and with this,
> the great mistake of applying the child to the breast on every
> occasion of its crying, without investigating the causing of its
> complaint, and under the belief that it wants food, putting
> the nipple into its crying mouth . . .[27]

Overfeeding was likely to be a more serious problem with bottle-fed babies because the mother did not have to take time out from her household duties to quiet the crying child and was not limited by the food supply available.

The problem of infant feeding was further complicated by the practice of feeding the infant solid foods too soon. In spite of the many warnings against this practice of giving the child food other than breast milk in its early months, the practice was bound in tradition and was still very strong. Reflecting this, Mrs. Beeton encouraged mothers that

The advantage to the mother of early accustoming the child to artificial food is as considerable to herself as beneficial to her infant; the demand on her physical strength in the first instance will be less severe and exhausting, the child will sleep longer on a less rapidly digestible ailment, and yield to both more quiet nights, and the mother will be more at liberty to go out for business or pleasure, another means of sustenance being at hand till her return. Besides these advantages, a judicious blending of the two systems of feeding, the infant will acquire greater constitutional strength, so that, if attacked by sickness or disease, it will have a much greater chance of resisting its virulence than if dependent alone on the mother, whose milk, affected by fatigue and the natural anxiety of the parent of her offspring, is at such a time neither good in its properties nor likely to be beneficial to the patient.[28]

Some of the foods that were given to infants were arrowroot, bread, flour, baked flour, farinaceous foods, oatmeal.

The results of these two common errors, overfeeding and premature use of solid foods, were often very serious. The infant suffered from distension and endured great pain and cried more and more. Those who were fortunate vomited the excess but many would have to endure the pain and then be subject to physic. Some of the food supplements caused serious diarrhea, as reported by Dr. Bakewell. He lamented that

When I see the ordinary practice of a nursery, and the want of common sense that seems to reign there — even among the better educated classes — I am astonished, not that such numbers *die*, but that any live! It was but a day or two ago that a lady consulted me about her infant, seven weeks old who was suffering from diarrhea. On inquiry what had been given it I was told that . . . she had given it oatmeal. She could hardly believe that oatmeal caused the diarrhoea.[29]

No doubt a number of middle-class children died from diarrhea, either because of food supplement, or more commonly from being dosed with an aperient or purgative which was too strong for their delicate constitutions. Thousands of children died from diarrhea every year, and the middle class had some share in this. In fact the class was caught rather uncomfortably between a desire for innovation and persistent traditionalism, all within the framework of a desire to do better for infants than ever before.

The most serious general problem the middle-class mother encountered in caring for her child concerned what to do during illness. Ignorance and tradition certainly reigned supreme here, but again there was a desire to change, if often misguided; hence the growing use of medicines such as purgatives and aperients. Dr. Bakewell pointed out that 'in ninety-nine out of every hundred cases, the maternal physician has not the remotest idea what is really the matter with the child, or what is really required for it, and gives the medicine entirely hap-hazard.'[30] Dr. Tilt made the same observation, in noting that

> Domestic mismanagement during illness is another not uncommon cause of death in infancy. Many mothers are continuously administering medicines of one kind or another and thereby derange instead of promoting the healthy operation of the infant system. Such persons never stop for a moment to inquire what the *cause* is, whether it has been or can be removed, or whether its removal will not of itself be sufficient to restore health . . . we have no hesitation in expressing our conviction that a child can encounter few greater dangers than that of being subjected to the vigorous discipline of a medicine-giving mother. . .[31]

The problem of treating illness in infants and children was essentially the same as was noted in the earlier section on general health. There was a heavy reliance on quack medicines. However, the consequences of this practice was graver for the child because its system was too fragile for most of these patent cure-alls. Dr. Joseph Morris, in an article entitled 'The Use of Soothing Syrups' described the problem. He wrote:

> There are few medical men in general practice who cannot call to mind numerous instances of children who have from time to time come under their care in an emaciated helpless condition, brought about by the constant pernicious use of quack medicines, known as 'soothing syrups'. Nor can we wonder that poor ignorant mothers should have recourse to such baneful remedies, when the proprietors of these patent drugs can find qualified medical men ready to eulogize the vendors by flaming testimonials of the marvelous efficacy of the nostrums in any and every disease, and will stand by them in open court when the wholesale use of such medicines is called into question.[32]

Among the more popular soothing compounds were Mrs. Winslow's Soothing Syrup, more commonly called 'Quietness,' Dalby's Carminative, and Godfrey's Cordial. All of these compounds contained opiates. It was reported that '*three-fourths* of all the deaths that take place from opium or its compounds occur in children under five years of age.'[33]

In fact, the problem was more serious yet, for drugs played a role in the shocking number of children who died yearly from convulsions and teething. For example, in 1847 23,347 children under five died from convulsions and 4,534 died from teething;[34] between 1873 and 1876 convulsions accounted for 16.3 per cent of the deaths in children under one year, ranking as the third largest cause of infant mortality. Convulsions continued to be a major source of death for young children throughout the century. Teething, a very natural process, accounted for 2 per cent of the deaths reported. In both categories, many of the deaths were caused by an overdose of drugs, as suggested by Dr. Morris, who concluded his article on soothing syrups with the following remark: 'May not the use of these syrups so frequent in the present day account for many of the deaths in children on whom inquests were held, and where deaths are returned as convulsions, etc.?'[35] Another article, entitled 'The Propriety of Giving Medicines to Children' was far more direct. It warned mothers that

> All kinds of narcotics — spirits, opium, and poppy, and
> quack medicines that contain these are thus dangerous,
> and their use should therefore invariably be renounced.
> The physician is often able to trace the origin of
> convulsions, or diseases terminating in water on the brain,
> to their use, and every day observes the nervous mischief
> they produce.[36]

Dr. Weatherly was also convinced that these medicines caused serious damage and often death. On the subject of teething he wrote that 'The rampant abuse of sedatives . . . during the teething period, is one I must call out against. Who can tell how many children are sent to their last home by the administration of those vile soothing powders and syrups.' He went on to emphasize that

> Supposing even that these 'cordials' and 'soothing potions'
> do not give rise to actual stupor, it is certain that they
> cause a congested condition of the brain, and conduce in
> a great measure to infantile convulsions and digestive and
> nervous disturbances. Often lasting during the natural life
> of the poor thing who is drugged by these patent medicines,
> which, while they seem to make the fortunes of many, are
> undoubtedly the course of frightful infant mortality.[37]

However, mothers were not given much help in management during illness, for doctors were guilty of the same gross ignorance. An article on 'Physics and Infancy' illustrated the situation that confronted many parents in telling the following story:

> 'Ah! poor thing, its gone at last,' said a fond father to a
> friend, alluding to the death of a baby two months old,
> 'but we did all we could for it, and there's no use repining.
> It was only ill a week, and during that time we had four

doctors, who gave it eight calomel powders, applied one
leech to the chest, one blister to the chest, six mustard
plasters, and gave it antimony wine and other medicines in
abundance. Yet the poor thing died!' The friend in amaze-
ment replied, 'Died! It would have been a miracle if it had
lived.'[38]

It is difficult to say when women sought medical attention for a sick
child. Judging from the mortality rates it would appear that it was not
often enough or soon enough. Traditional ideas about childhood illnesses
were still very strong, as indicated by Dr. Bakewell in his last article on
infant mortality. His warning was that

I would caution my readers against the notion, too prevalent
among mothers, that ailments will get well of themselves
when the child has cut all its teeth. Very frequently we see
children suffering from scrofulous and other constitutional
diseases, who are undergoing no treatment, because their
mothers 'fancy' it is nothing but the teeth.[39]

He also noted that many children died of bronchitis because their
mothers failed to take them to a physician soon enough. Mothers
ignorant of the disease treated it as a cold, but even a delay of twenty-
four hours could make the case hopeless because of the rapid progress
of the disease in infants.[40] But in many cases even when a doctor's
advice was sought it was of little use, because of the lack of
knowledge of pediatric care. Traditionalism and the state of medical
practice supplemented each other.

Hence the growing concern about children's health enhanced
anxieties on the mothers' part and at the same time, in public discussions,
produced a barrage of criticisms of maternal care. Not yet would the
concern produce the kind of knowledge about the infant's health and
care that was needed. As with the advice on women's health, the advice
for child care was too general, based in fact on the same three principles
of general health: regulation of diet, proper clothing and plenty of fresh
air and exercise. There was little concrete assistance for the mother
faced with serious illness and the prospect of frequent infant death. The
middle-class mother, no longer resigned to infant mortality, had to feel
an acute sense of helplessness and frustration when she realized that
despite her efforts an intentions the fate of her child was still so very
precarious.

Along with the growing concern for the physical health of the child
a profound interest developed in securing the child's mental and moral
health. Here too a new attitude toward children was beginning to make
strong inroads among the middle-class by mid-century and was to alter
child-rearing methods significantly by the end of the century. The child
was beginning to be viewed as an individual with very particular needs

108

which only a loving mother could fulfill. The ramifications of this new concept of the child for the Victorian mother was indeed great, as they increased her responsibilities to the child even more.

The manuals provide us with some insight into the qualitative changes in child-rearing which reflect this new attitude of the child as an individual. As early as the 1830s it was felt that the future happiness of the adult was mainly dependent on its happiness as a child. The sentiment expressed was that

> ... the forming of the minds of children in that early stage of their existence which, in nine cases out of every ten, determines their quality, character, and usefulness, through the whole period of life, is the most sacred duty which devolves upon the sex, and if they neglect this, or perform it in an improper manner, the character of the whole of society is lowered to the same extent ... nor after education can repair injury done here, neither can any adverse circumstance in after life altogether destroy the advantages which result from the early bias given to the mind by the judicious attention of a really good mother.[41]

The concept of happiness in childhood was to begin in the cradle, and this quickly resulted in a novel and extensive discussion of crying babies. Traditionally, it was believed that it was good and natural that a child cry. However, early in the century a growing challenge to this common practice developed. Mothers were urged that children only cry for one reason — they are uncomfortable — and thus they should make the early period of the child's life as 'easy' as possible. 'Happy Infancy' was as important as a 'happy childhood.'[42]

In order to insure a happy infancy and a happy childhood the mother had to be intimately related to the child. She had to know its every cry and what it meant. The mother was advised to be as indulgent as possible; not to be irritated by children's faults, but to pity their weaknesses. She was told to allow them to be gay and familiar before her, as that she might know their real disposition. Love was the foundation for this intimate relationship. The general philosophy expressed was that

> The great agent in executing family law is love. This should manifest itself in words, looks, and tones, to be properly effective. The parent whose cold and repulsive manner represses all confiding familiarity in the child, is building a wall of ice between himself and his offspring ... the child should be early taught to confide his feelings freely to his parents, by the open and loving manner of the parent, or he will seek companions and confidants elsewhere.[43]

The qualitative change in attitude toward children and their particular needs prompted a wide discussion over discipline. Mothers were constantly writing for advice on this particular problem, indicating that they were deeply concerned about the changing concepts and that, on this point, the advice literature was reflecting their real problems. A typical inquiry read as follows: 'A Young Mother requests that we will give her our opinion on the best means of correcting children's behaviour between the ages of one and three years, and how to obtain prompt obedience without too much severity.'[44] The debate over discipline grew quite intense with the years, reaching its peak in the late 1860s. The long and heated discussion over the question of personal chastisement of children which appeared in *The Englishwoman's Domestic Magazine* (*EDM*) from 1868-70 illustrated the perplexity of this problem for parents. By the third quarter of the century it was a fairly well-accepted principle of child care that the mother direct the child positively, through love, kindness, and a soft manner. Physical chastisement was to be rarely employed, and only when all else failed. A practical illustration of how the mother was to implement the positive approach to discipline is seen in the following recommendations:

> When children touch objects that they should not, it's natural, the child should be taught to yield up what would be injurious . . . In order to facilitate the acquisition, never allow anything to be taken from it without immediately supplying its place with some other attractive object; but as prevention is better than cure, you must avoid placing within its reach what it ought not to have. Try to make compliance with your wish pleasant to its feeling, by often requiring it to do what you know will provide pleasure.[45]

In much of the new advice given to the mother on child-rearing the buds of modern child psychology were beginning to break through; for example, *The Family Friend* suggested in an article that the mother put herself in the child's position. She must learn to be patient with the child because its attention span was short.[46] Another clear indication of the new attitude toward children was found in the following reflection of children's nature. It observed that

> In some families, the children are continually addressed as 'tiresome plagues,' 'mischievous little brats,' and such-like terms. In some families, the children are considered to be very good, if they do not jump, sing, shout, or make a noise, and are grave and sedate as penguins. But this is in direct opposition to nature! Such very good children are very much to be pitied.[47]

True, it is difficult to say how widespread these new attitudes were. Yet they seemed threatening enough to rouse considerable criticism from the traditionalists. As one critic of the changes lamented,

> ... the tendency of this age is to laxness in family
> government and this is one of our great dangers. In some
> circles, 'training up a child in the way he should go' is
> becoming obsolete. Parents let their children grow wild
> instead of training them; or, if they take some pains, they
> yield more than required. While they pretend to hold the
> reigns, the children continue to coax or tease them out of
> their hands more than half the time. They virtually obey,
> oftener, than they exclusively command.[48]

The transition to the new disciplinary modes was clearly through
middle-class mothers. What role did the Victorian father play in family
government? It is quite apparent that our image of the Victorian father
as the autocratic despot is just that — an image. The growing emphasis
was on concomitant relationship between the husband and wife,
especially concerning the rearing of children; for example, it was often
heard that 'both parents should understand this; the mother should
second the authority of the father, while the father should always
support the power of the mother.'[49] However, in reality the father
played little role in the everyday affairs of child-rearing, simply because
he did not have the time. This was suggested in Mrs. Ellis' remark that

> Fathers of families, in the present day, and the fact cannot
> be acknowledged without serious regret, are for the most
> part, too deeply engaged in the pursuit of objects widely
> differing in their nature from those which belong to the
> moral discipline of home; and therefore, it becomes more
> the duty of the mothers, especially those of the middle class
> of society, to look beyond the things of the moment, to
> consider the almost double responsibility which devolves
> upon them, and to inquire earnestly into the probable
> means of assuring the future good of their children.[50]

The extent to which parental discipline changed must remain
uncertain until we have more studies on actual child-rearing patterns.
The implications of the manuals are clear, but we will need a break-
through to new kinds of sources if we are to determine the extent of
their implementation. But discussions of new disciplinary patterns
complement the obvious increase in the attachment toward the
individual child, which dominated the concern for physical well-being
from infancy onwards. This change left the middle-class mother
extremely vulnerable. New disciplinary patterns might prove successful,
but their novelty assured a difficult transition; it was surely easier to go
by fixed rules than by the individual personality of the child. And the
sheer anxiety over the child's health — admittedly counterproductive
at times — was immense. The Victorian mother was not only giver of
life, but also maintainer of life, teacher to her children, confidant and

disciplinarian. She had to devote a great deal of her time and energy to the fulfillment of this complex role.

The sense that the burdens of motherhood increased with the middle class involves a final and very important question — the size of her family. If the Victorian woman continued to have the traditional number of children, if would be virtually impossible to implement the changes in child-rearing because they demanded increased and elaborate care for each and every child. It was in this situation that the Victorian family began to reduce its birth rate. This fact itself is familiar, but it needs reinterpretation in light of an understanding of the complexities of the role of motherhood. Who made the decision to reduce births, when, and by what means, all demand careful investigation.

Notes

1. Dr. Alfred Fennings, *Every Mother's Book*, title page.
2. Dr. R. Hall Bakewell, 'Infant Mortality, and Its Causes,' in *The British Mothers' Journal* (June, 1857), p. 141. The other instalment series ran from June to December in the series. Further reference to the series will give specific date.
3. *The Mothers' Friend* (London, 1861), advertisement.
4. Harrison, *The Early Victorians*, pp. 2-3.
5. *England: Causes of the 420,977 Deaths Registered in the Year 1847*, published by the Registrar General (London, 1851).
6. *The Mothers' Companion*, vol. iv (1890), p. 30
7. Ansell, *On the Rate of Mortality,* Table V, p. 71.
8. The findings are derived from information found in the following volumes of the *Annual Report of the Registrars General of Births, Deaths, Marriage,* (Vol. LI (1864),·p. 425, Vol. lxxxvi (1884-5), pp. 5, 63
9. 'How to Manage a Baby,' in *The British Mothers' Journal* (June 1858), p.135.
10. Bakewell, 'Infant Mortality and its Causes' (June 1857), p. 141.
11. Dr. E. Lankester, 'Plain Rules for the Management of Infants,' in *The London Medical Record* (4 March, 1874), p. 127.
12. Conquest, *Letters to a Mother*, pp. 92-3.
13. Allbutt, *Every Mothers' Handbook*, pp. 50-57.
14. Conquest, *Letters to a Mother*, p. 94.
15. Tilt, *The Elements of Health*, p. 42.
16. Banks and Banks, *Feminism*, p. 68.
17. Dr. Lionel Weatherly, *The Young Wife's Own Book: A Manual of Personal and Family Hygiene, Containing Everything that the Young Wife and Mother Ought to Know, Concerning her own Health and that of Her Children at the Most Important Periods of Life* (London, 1882), p. 119.
18. Jonathan Gathorne-Hardy, *The Rise and Fall of the British Nanny* (London, 1972), p. 42.
19. Tilt, *The Elements of Health*, p. 47.
20. *The Mother's Medical Adviser* (London, 1843), p. 8.
21. *The British Mother's Journal for 1857* (November, 1857), pp. 248-9.
22. *The Family Friend*, Vol. IV (1851), p. 321.
23. 'A New Food For Infants,' *The Englishwoman's Domestic Magazine*, Vol. VI (April 1869), p. 185

24. Bull, *Hints to Mothers* (1877 ed.), p. 40.
25. Beeton, *Household Management*, pp. 1034-5.
26. *The Englishwoman's Domestic Magazine*, Vol. VII (1859), p. 243.
27. Beeton, *Household Management*, p. 1037.
28. Ibid., pp. 1038-9.
29. Bakewell, 'Infant Mortality, and Its Causes', (December 1857). p. 27.
30. Bakewell, 'Infant Mortality, and its Causes' (October 1857), p. 221.
31. Tilt, *The Elements of Health*, pp. 85-6.
32. Dr. Joseph Morris, 'The Use of Soothing Syrups,' in *The British Medical Journal*, Vol. II (30 October 1875), p. 570.
33. Bull, *Hints to Mothers* (1877 ed.), p. 296.
34. *England: Causes of the 420,977 Deaths Registered in the Year 1847*, published by the Registrar General (London, 1851).
35. Morris, 'The Use of Soothing Syrups,' p. 570.
36. 'The Propriety of Giving Medicines to Children', in *The British Mothers' Journal of 1859* (April 1859), p. 84.
37. Weatherly, *The Young Wife's Own Book*, p. 154.
38. 'Physics and Infancy,' in *The Family Economist*, Vol. I (1848), p. 96.
39. Bakewell, 'Infant Mortality, and Its Causes,' (December, 1857), p. 274.
40. Ibid., p. 275.
41. 'Women in Domestic Life', in *The Magazine of Domestic Economy*, Vol. I (1835-6), p. 67.
42. 'On the Early Management of Children,' in *The Magazine of Domestic Economy*, Vol. I (1835-6), p. 123.
43. Rev. T.V. Moore, 'The Family as Government', in *The British Mothers' Journal* (May 1856), p. 99.
44. 'Answer to a Young Mother's Queries – Obedience a Habit – Obedience a Virtue', in *The British Mother's Magazine*, Vol. V (June 1849), p. 137.
45. Ibid., p. 137.
46. *The Family Friend* (1858-9), p. 259.
47. *The Family Friend* (1848), p. 157.
48. 'The Parental Submission,' in *The British Mother's Family Magazine for 1864* (July 1864), p. 163.
49. 'On the Importance of Parental Consistency and Cooperation', in *The British Mothers' Journal for 1857* (June 1857), p. 136.
50. Ellis, *The Mothers of England*, p. 37.

7 MIDDLE-CLASS WOMEN AND BIRTH CONTROL – A PERSONAL TRIUMPH

The deliberate limitation of family size was one of the principal contributions of middle-class women to the modernization process of women generally. This decision flowed not only from the new definitions of childhood and motherhood; it represented the only means available in the mid-nineteenth century of resolving several key problems arising from the new situation and new consciousness of women. As manager of the household the middle-class woman, confronted with limited means, was acutely aware of the expenses involved in maintaining her children in the new fashion. Also birth control was the most practical means of coping with the unresolved problems of maternal mortality.

The positive aspects of the decision to control births were perhaps the most compelling for the middle-class woman. As we will see, the middle-class woman's new image of self involved a new sexuality – one of more intense personal enjoyment. In order to maximize sexual enjoyment, it was necessary to prevent the traditional consequences of sex – pregnancy. Through the adoption of birth control the middle-class woman found the most important ingredient to liberation.

It might seem obvious to go from this list of factors to an examination of the means by which the middle-class woman emancipated herself. However it is necessary first to discuss the historical debate surrounding the population question. The controversy over the British population has waxed long and occasionally hot, but to date it has produced only superficial levels of understanding with regard to the limitation of births. As we will see it totally misrepresents the role of the middle class in the adoption of birth control. It errs in chronology and motivation. It completely ignores also the role of women or relegates them, once again, to the role of passive instruments of the male will.

The framework for any investigation of the demographic history of the period is that between the 1850s and 1870s the English fertility rate rose to new heights. The maximum birth rate for this period was in 1876. Then suddenly in 1877 the birth rate began to decline, and this continued until the 1920s.[1] Thus 1877, the first year to reflect a decline in the crude birth rate, became a watershed in the British population controversy, for the obvious question was: what caused the sudden shift? The theorizing about the dramatic decline has stimulated some interesting postulates, with the most important discussion centering on the claim that adoption of birth control practices was the major cause for the decline.

One of the first explanations put forward for the sudden decline in the birth rate was the Bradlaugh-Besant trial of 1877-8. Due to the coincidence in timing, many have considered this famous trial, which involved the publication of birth control literature, to be the major cause behind the demographic shift.[2] The supporters of the Bradlaugh-Besant thesis contend that through the publicity of this trial birth control information was made available, for the first time, to a wide public. However, it is doubtful whether the case played any significant role in the decline of the birth rate and the widespread adoption of birth control practices. The result of Bradlaugh-Besant merely signified that birth control was widely recognized and accepted by this time. Its impact could not have been so quickly felt. The trial was set up as a test case to establish the legality of publishing birth control literature, which had been going on peacefully throughout the century until this one incident.[3] The case accomplished this, but little more can be attributed to it. That it continues to be invoked as an explanation of a massive social change suggests the superficiality of much of the inquiry to date.

Many accounts have seized upon economics as being the determining factor in the decline of the British birth rate and this is clearly a more promising approach. In the late nineteenth century, poverty was considered the force behind the adoption of birth control practices. This explanation follows from the Malthusian promptings so common during the century, especially those of the Neo-Malthusian League of the 1880s. However, scholars as early as the turn of the century — for example, Newsholme and Stevenson in 1906 — noted that the classes practising birth control were not victims of poverty and thus the standard of living thesis was advanced. This position claimed that the decline in the birth rate was related to the general advance in material conditions and expressed a popular determination to maintain their improved living standards.[4]

With time, however, students of the birth control phenomenon began to turn to a number of causes rather than relying on a single explanation. This was the position of Norman Himes in his classic work *Medical History of Contraception*,[5] published in 1936, and the *Report of the Royal Commission on Population*,[6] of June 1949. According to the Commission, the widespread adoption of family limitation in the 1870s was due to the following: a decay of the family handicraft system and the rise of large-scale industry and factory organization, the loss of security and the growth of competitive individualism, the relative decline in agriculture and the rise in importance of industry and commerce with their related shift to urbanization from the country-side, the growing prestige of science and the declining influence of religion, the development of popular education and of higher standards of living, the growth of humanitarianism and the emancipation of women. Corresponding to these various new motives, the development of new and better birth control methods provided the means whereby control was possible. The cumulative effect of these causes plus the 'special jolt' which the 1875 depression and the Bradlaugh-Besant trial of 1877-8 gave to the public were responsible for the decline in the birth rate.[7]

While the single factor theories continue to appear too simple, the multi-factor thesis is just as ineffective in explaining the decline because it does not sort out priorities in the various causes; almost anything can be involved. In both approaches, however, the two factors of economics and the Bradlaugh-Besant trial remained dominant in accounting for the decline. These factors have gained even wider acceptance since the work of Professor Joseph A. Banks, which provided a persuasive and readable overview of the birth rate decline that has not been seriously challenged since its appearance. In his book, *Prosperity and Parenthood*, Banks sets forth the thesis that by 1877 the economic situation was such that it was becoming increasingly difficult for the middle class to maintain its standard of living. In order to control their living situation, the middle class now found it necessary to limit the size of its family.[8] According to Banks, the Bradlaugh-Besant case was the 'catalytic agent' which made available the means to limit one's family and thereby maintain the established standard of living. The key point — indeed the only really novel aspect — of the Banks' thesis is his claim that since economics was the determining factor in limiting the size of the family, it was therefore the exclusive decision of the husband to initiate birth control practice. In a later work, *Feminism and Family Planning*,[9] written with his wife, the Banks' defend further the position that the woman played no role in the decision-making process concerning birth control by discounting the effect of the women's rights movement of the nineteenth century on married women's lives. The position that the women's movement of the day was primarily concerned with the plight of the single woman is indeed accurate. However to conclude from this that women therefore did not play any role in the decision-making process concerning birth control is simplistic. The Banks' position that the Victorian wife dutifully submitted to bearing her husband's children before 1870 and dutifully submitted to his decision to prevent conception after 1870 is not at all clear from the evidence given.

In this case, as in others, the real situation confronting the middle-class woman has been misrepresented. In the first place, the chronology is simply wrong for the middle class. The middle class has been buried in the general population statistics. It should be obvious that relatively small population groups such as the middle class may have begun birth control before the 1870s; the 1870s in fact, reveal the spread of the

116

birth control ethic to much larger population groups. The middle-class leadership in birth control practices was as true in England as on the European continent, and the class was well acquainted with the practice of birth control before 1877, as will be shown shortly. And thus, as we have contended, the Bradlaugh-Besant case was not a 'catalytic agent' but a mere reflection of accomplished facts; and the economic factor must be reconsidered in the light of a new chronology.[10] It was shown earlier in the section on budgets that the middle class always had an economic problem. There was nothing dramatically new in their economic circumstances in 1877. Also since the woman did play an important role in the economic planning of the family, her participation in the decision-making process concerning birth control cannot be ignored. If one looks at the problem from the Victorian woman's point of view, one sees that her role in the decision to limit the number of children she bore was indeed crucial.

From a comparative standpoint, the conventional analysis of British developments seems debatable. The 1877 date, for example, seems quite late when we know that the French urban middle class began to cut their birth rate early in the nineteenth century,[11] and the German urban middle class, though quite new to industrial society, at least by the 1870s. Was the British middle class so different? The only general data on fertility and class trends for nineteenth-century England is the 'Report on the Fertility of Marriage,' published as Volume 13 of the 1911 census of England and Wales, which gives some data on the second half of the nineteenth century. There are no data permitting more than guesswork on the situation prior to the 1850s. However, the 1911 Report showed clearly that in the 1860s the middle class was restricting the number of children it had, and as we will see, some segments of the class were practicing birth control as early as the 1850s. The census Report was based on a sample of 2,086,010 married women over 45 whose husbands also survived to this age. The population was divided into eight social classes: Class I – Upper Professional; Class II – Lower Professional; Class III – Skilled Laborer; Class IV – Semi-Skilled Laborer; Class V – Unskilled Laborer; Class VI – Textile Worker; Class VII – Miner; Class VIII – Agricultural Laborer. For the purpose of this study Class I and Class II are most important. The Table gives the 1911 findings on completed fertility for these two classes.

Thus it can be seen that there were substantial decreases in the birth rate for both classes even though the peak was yet to come in the 1860s. The data for Class I prior to 1861 is rather vague because it is based on less than a hundred wives. However, Class II, which is the most relevant for a study of the bulk of the middle class, showed a decisive decrease of 3.8 per cent in the 1850s. Admittedly, the small sample available by 1911 of marriages begun before 1861 makes this evidence suggestive only. But in combination with the qualitative evidence that will be discussed later in the chapter, there is a strong likelihood that middle-class birth control was under way by mid-century if not a bit before that, although the process was accentuated by the 1870s.

TABLE X

Completed Fertility per 100 Wives by Social Class

Date of Marriage	Class I	% Decrease	Class II	% Decrease
1851 or earlier	605		728	
1851 – 1861	625	3.3	700	-3.8
1861 – 1871	593	-5.1	650	-7.1
1871 – 1881	497	-16.2	567	-12.1
1881 – 1886	422	-15.1	493	-13.0

Source: *Census of England and Wales, 1911*, 'Report on the Fertility of Marriage,' Part II, Table XLIV, p. xcviii.

A study made by J.W. Innes of the 1911 Fertility Report attempted to determine more precisely the changes in fertility patterns among the classes.[12] In his study, Innes split Class I and II into the following subdivisions: Class I-A – Upper Professional, which was composed of army, navy and marine officers, clergymen, barristers, solicitors, physicians, surgeons, registered medical practitioners, authors, editors, journalists, reporters, civil mining engineers, architexts; Class I-B – Lower Professional, civil service officers, clerks, law clerks, dentists, schoolmasters, teachers, professors, lecturers, persons engaged in scientific pursuits, accountants; Class II-A – Upper Commercial, brokers, agent factors, commercial travellers, auctioneers, appraisers, valuers, house agents, bankers, bank and insurance officials, or business clerks; Class II-B – Lower Commercial – shopkeepers and their assitants, Class II-C – Farmers.[13] According to the definition of middle class used for this study the significant groups are Class I-B, Class II-A, and Class II-B. Because of the nature of the sample before the 1860s, which was limited by its size, as noted above, Innes was only able to begin with the 1860s for his more detailed breakdown of class trends. Table XI reports Innes' findings for Classes I-B, II-A, and Class II-B.

The breakdown of fertility rates according to occupations found in Table XI indicates two significant points. The clearest correlation between lower fertility and occupation was in the newer professions and those professions most advanced in the modernization process. Engineers, doctors and barristers ranked among the lowest, whereas traditional occupations such as the clergy and commercial interests

118

TABLE XI

Completed Fertility Rates Per 100 Wives in Sub-Groups of Classes I and II,
For Marriage Age Quinquennia and All Marriages Standardized

Marriage Age	Date	Class I-B	% Decrease	Class II-A	% Decrease	Class II-B	% Decrease
15 – 19	1861-1871	779		719		805	
15 – 19	1871-1881	600	-21.7	641	-10.8	722	-10.3
15 – 19	1881-1886	508	-15.3	562	-12.3	644	-10.8
20 – 24	1861-1871	653		642		677	
20 – 24	1871-1881	504	-22.8	523	-18.5	579	-14.4
20 – 24	1881-1886	415	-17.6	442	-15.4	501	-13.2
25 – 29	1861-1871	513		517		518	
25 – 29	1871-1881	413	-19.5	423	-18.2	451	-12.9
25 – 29	1881-1886	342	-17.2	353	-16.5	382	-18.1
25 – 29	1886-1891	295	-16.7	306	-13.3	341	-10.7
30 – 34	1861-1871	369		393		373	
30 – 34	1871-1881	332	-10.1	309	-21.4	328	-12.0
30 – 34	1881-1886	264	-20.4	260	-15.8	278	-15.2
30 – 34	1886-1891	238	-12.8	232	-10.7	251	-10.4
30 – 34	1891-1896	187	-18.7	196	-15.5	225	-10.4
Standardized	1861-1871	620		604		639	
	1871-1881	484	-21.9	503	-16.8	555	-13.2
	1881-1886	401	-17.2	428	-14.9	481	-13.3
	1861-1886		-35.2		-29.2		-23.6

Source: Innes, *Class Fertility Trends*, p. 60. Rates were computed from data supplied by Table 35, 'Fertility Report', Part II, pp. 98-143.

ranked the highest.   Within the commercial profession bankers, with a rate of 321, had a markedly lower rate than the commercial profession in general which was composed mainly of shopkeepers and other traditional groups. One sees also that the relationship between economic pressure and birth control was at best very ambiguous. Again engineers, despite a high rate of economic success, limited births earlier than declining professions. If one was to argue that economic pressure was the predominant concern, one would expect law clerks and solicitors to have a lower rate than the barristers. But such was not the case. These points confirm more fully the thesis of this study, that modernization with its new mentality is the more important factor in explaining the sudden decline in births.[14]

These data clearly indicate that the middle class was practising birth control well before the economic slow-down of the late 1870s, with certain major segments in the lead. This revision of the conventional chronology is abundantly confirmed by looking at the rate of female fertility for the middle-class community of Camberwell in the period 1851-71 and then comparing it to London's rate for the same period.

TABLE XII

Completed Fertility per 100 Wives by
Husband's Occupation

Profession	Completed Fertility
Local Administrator	431
Insurance Agent	415
Other Clergy	415
Anglican Clergy	391
Commercial & Business Clerks	385
Post Office Clerks	379
Accountants	372
Law Clerks	371
Civil Servants	369
Merchants	367
Dentists	365
School Teachers	357
Solicitors	352
Architects	349
Physicians	328
Navy Officers	323
Bankers	321
Engineers	321
Barristers	308

Source: *Census of England and Wales, 1911*, 'Report on the Fertility of Marriage,' Part II, Table XLVII, p. lv, Table 36, pp. 145-6.

TABLE XIII

Fertility per 1000 Females Aged 20-44

	1851-1861	1861-1871
Camberwell	1.23	1.15
London	1.41	1.51

Source: *Annual Registrar General's Report of Births, Deaths, Marriages,* Vol. XVII (1862), pp. 196-200; Vol. XVI (1884-5), pp. 236-40.

The above table illustrates two important findings. First Camberwell's fertility rate declined 7 per cent in the twenty years, whereas London's rate increased by 7 per cent. Second, comparison of the two communities shows marked difference in fertility patterns. In the first period, 1851-61, Camberwell's fertility rate was 15 per cent lower than London's. In the second period the divergence between a middle-class community and a general urban population was even more noticeable, with Camberwell's fertility rate 30 per cent under that of London's. In the case of Camberwell we can actually pinpoint the year in which a particular middle-class decision to limit its birth rate was made, for, in 1855 there was an absolute decline in births despite a continuous influx into the suburb. Undoubtedly more local and class-specific studies would be desirable but they can only confirm the fact that beneath national demographic patterns the middle class, and particularly its most modern segments, switched to birth control by mid-century.[15]

This means among other things that no single economic explanation can account for the decision, for the 1850s constituted a period of unusually consistent prosperity. And once we realize that we cannot explain either the chronology of birth control efforts or the differentiation of such efforts within the middle class by economic crisis, the whole question of the role of women in the birth control process is reopened. As we noted at the outset, middle-class women had compelling reasons to limit the birth rate. The mounting concern over health, particularly the health of the mother, and the growing desire of women to gain control over their personal being could easily influence the decision to limit family size. So could the new sense of obligation to the individual child.

The literature of the day offered some strong evidence that these aspects were indeed of profound importance and that women were entering the decision-making process on this basis. As early as the 1820s parents were urged to limit the size of their families, not so much for economic reasons but for the health and happiness of the family. The following sentiment was often expressed:

There is an ill-founded notion current, that to reproduce an
unlimited number of children is beneficial to society. It is
only a benefit to children to be produced when they can be
made healthy and happy. It is only a benefit to parents
when they can produce them with the preservation of their
own health and happiness. It is an evil when they become a
burthen to pre-existing members; an evil when they become
a burthen to the parents.[16]

Apparently this was the attitude that made strong inroads into the
middle-class life style and produced the demographic shift within the
class. Certainly by 1870, the attitude toward large families was critical
and unsympathetic. The following statement from a book, *Beauty is
Power*, written to encourage large families again, noted the hostility of
the day:

The days have long gone by when to be the fruitful mother
of children was the happiest ambition to which, in public
estimation, a woman could aspire; and certainly there is no
longer any necessary connection between the fate of a
family increasing and multiplying, and that of its possessing
the land. If it is still considered rather undignified to have
no children at all, it is looked upon as supremely ridiculous
to have a great many. The bare mention of 'a full quiver' is
enough to upset the gravity of an entire company.[17]

In an extreme of the dominant trend, Dr. Elizabeth Blackwell, in her
work *How to Keep a Household in Health*, went so far as to suggest
that children were not a necessary part of marriage. She stated that "I
do not consider, as it is so often stated, that the great object of marriage
is to produce children; marriage has higher humanitarian objects."[18]

An important consideration in the discussions on family size was the
health of the mother. Austin Holyoake, in his often-quoted work *Large
or Small Families*? was quite emphatic about the debilitating effects of
too many children on the woman's health. He noted that

The mother of a numerous progeny risks her life eight or
ten times, besides passing the best portion of her existence
in a continual suffering. A grave charge made by opponents
is, that to check the population is an 'abnormality', and
must impair the health of both man and woman. This is not
true; but if it were it would be easy to show that the ailments
forced upon women in a 'natural' way far exceed any
possible arise from an exercise of prudence.[19]

The medical profession stressed over and over again the importance of
spacing pregnancies on the grounds of conserving the mother's health.
Our previous discussion of nursing showed that as early as the 1840s,
doctors were warning mothers of the debilitating effects of too frequent

pregnancies.

Thus there is substantial indication, as reflected in the literature of the day, that the well-being of the woman was an important consideration in the decision to limit family size. In order to test this thesis fully it is necessary to examine the means by which the middle class was able to control its family size and what role the woman played in this process. Here we encounter another dilemma. There were, in the nineteenth century, a number of methods available to those wishing to prevent conception: abstinence, *coitus interruptus*, abortion, use of the 'safe period' and a variety of contraceptive devices. We will probably never be able to determine which method of birth control was most commonly practised in the nineteenth century. But historians up to this point have reflected little uncertainty; abstinence and *coitus interruptus* have been assumed predominant. These are male methods, that require the husband to exert the control. But this ignores the possibility of co-operation between husband and wife. It ignores the other birth control methods that were widely known in the nineteenth century. And it rests on several dubious assumptions about a unique and rather unattractive picture of the Victorian personality. This last point must be considered before we deal — admittedly somewhat tentatively — with actual birth control methods.

It has been easy to assume that abstinence was widely practised because it has been easy to assume that the Victorian middle class was odd. The reliance on *coitus interruptus* and abstinence as prime methods of birth control seems to be based more on our image of the Victorian male as the self-controlled, strong-willed autocratic despot and the Victorian female as the submissive, sexless creature than on any specific evidence. But this misses at least two vital related points; first that family governance was probably more mutual than the despotic husband image allows and second that the sexual enjoyment was quite actively sought by both marriage partners. There was much discussion among the Victorians on the relationship of husband and wife. In the majority of the discussions the emphasis was always on the importance of co-operation between the two partners; marriage was viewed as a union of two equal parts. The philosophy was that

> ... what is fair for one is fair for the other. In the married
> state there should be the strictest equality. The husband
> must come down for the position of master, not that his
> place may be taken by the woman — but that she may be
> the sharer of his pleasure, hopes and joys as she has been the
> partaker of his pains, fears, and sorrow.[20]

Even the more tradition-bound writers such as the author of *The English Matron*, noted that marriage was never regarded as a state of servitude for women.[21] Mutual love and respect, confidence, frankness were all essential ingredients in a harmonious marriage.

This sense of mutuality and equality was carried through to the most intimate relationship between a husband and wife, their sex life. This was most explicit in Dr. Michael Ryan's discussions of marriage obligations — in a popular marriage manual — in which he noted that

> ... to preserve conjugal fidelity ... requires two things: — First, that the debt should be paid by one spouse to the other; and secondly, that it should be paid to this person alone. Both are equally bound to fulfill this obligation when the debt is demanded ... [22]

Admittedly, this is not conclusive evidence, but taken with the discussion of family matters thus far presented, in which the role of the woman was found to be very important indeed, it casts serious doubt on the conventional view. The abundance of evidence against the traditional image of the Victorian household, as a hierarchial structure with a despot at its head, presents an important challenge which cannot be ignored.

The second image — the Victorian woman as a sexless creature -- needs to be discussed in detail not only because it relates directly to the question of birth control, but also because the image has been so pervasive. The commonly cited evidence on female sexuality in the nineteenth century is the work of the reformist William Acton.[23] Book after book written about the Victorians quotes Acton as being representative of Victorian sex attitudes.[24] The following passage from Acton is familiar:

> Having taken pains to obtain and compare abundant evidence on the subject I should say that the majority of women (happily for them) are not very much troubled with sexual feelings of any kind. What men are habitually, women are only exceptionally ... there can be no doubt that sexual feeling in the female is in the majority of cases in abeyance ... and even if roused (which in many instance it can never be) compared with that of the male. As a general rule, a modest woman seldom desires any sexual gratification for herself. She submits to her husband, but only to please him; and but for the desire of maternity would far rather be relieved from his attentions.[25]

Was the middle-class woman as disinterested in sexual fulfilment as Acton indicated? It is indeed impossible to answer this question fully. Moments in the bedroom are not recorded for later observers. However, even the evidence presented thus far of a new image of self developing among middle-class women warrants that we at least attempt to deal with the question.

First we must realize that as far as evidence goes there is very little to support the image of the sexless female. Acton's impressions of female sexuality are almost useless. The above quote was one of only two passages in the entire discourse which talked of women. For the most part the book was devoted to men and male sexuality. Further, even Acton's contemporaries took exception to the above statement; for example, a review in *The London Medical Review* made the following objections:

> Sexual intercourse in marriage is a subject of vital importance, and one the bearing of which every medical man should be fully acquainted with. There is one statement of Mr. Acton's which we think is open to question, viz., that venereal pleasure is almost entirely on the side of the male. Now, this is unphysiological in the first place, and moreover, experience proves the contrary. . . there can be no doubt that both in the human subject and in the lower animals the female does participate fully in the sexual passion.[26]

And there were other voices on the topic of female sexuality in the nineteenth century which have not generally been heard. There is some evidence to suggest that the concept of female sexuality was beginning to be recognized as an important factor that needed fulfilment. One of the earliest statements made in defense of the woman's sexual needs was Richard Carlile's very outspoken work, *Every Woman's Book; Or, What is Love?*, first published in 1825. Carlile's philosophy was as follows:

> It is a barbarous custom that forbids the maid to make advances in love, or that confines these advances to the eye, the fingers, the gesture, the motion, the manner. It is equally absurd and ridiculous. Why should not the female state her passion to the male, as well as the male to the female? What impropriety can there be in it? What bad effect can it produce? Is it modest? Why is it immodest? Is it not virtuous? Why is it not virtuous? It would be difficult to find answers to these questions. Equality and the right to make advances, in all the affairs of genuine love, are claimed for the female. The hypocrisy, the cruelty that would stifle or disguise a passion, whether in the male or in the female is wicked, and should be exposed, reprobated, and detested. Young Women! Assume an equality, plead your passion when you feel it, plead it to those to whom it applies.[27]

Carlile recognized that 'every healthy woman after the age of puberty feels the passion of love. It is part of her health and is natural a consequence as hunger and thirst."[28] Admittedly, Carlile's position was by no means typical in the 1820s: as always, his thinking was well ahead of his time. There were, however, among the respected medical community, others who agreed in essence with his philosophy.

Dr. Elizabeth Blackwell spoke for the cause of female sexuality. In both her books, *The Human Element in Sex*,[29] and *Moral Education*,[30] she went to great lengths to emphasize that female sexuality was as strong as males. Dr. Ryan's statement on marriage obligations quoted above suggested that women had a right to sexual satisfaction.[31] Dr. Allbutt, in his book *The Wife's Handbook*, also made a similar statement. He noted that 'During connection both husband and wife should endeavor to be in a happy state of mind. The wife especially should have happy thoughts when having connection.'[32] Thus it can be seen that there were indeed voices other than Acton's on the subject of sex. This is not to imply that the discussion of middle-class sexual values is exhausted but to suggest that at the least, we need to re-evaluate many of our generalizations.

There is no denying that there was an influential element in the official middle-class culture which placed heavy restrictions on sex, especially for the middle-class adolescent. Young middle-class girls were to be chaste in body and mind until marriage. In the nineteenth century this became more and more difficult because middle-class girls were maturing sexually earlier, usually at age 14,[33] and marrying late, about age 25. Thus for about ten years they were forced to sublimate natural sexual drives. How did the middle-class girl cope with this problem? No doubt some took seriously the warnings about the vices of sex out of marriage, generally from the spokesmen of the religious community. One of the strongest sexual hang-ups of middle-class culture was masturbation. Girls were instructed that masturbation would lead to nervousness, depression, hysteria, senility, and she would bear weak and sickly children. In addition she would surely dull her sense of sexual enjoyment after marriage.[34] The last warning is especially significant because it illustrates an important point — that the famous middle-class sex ethic was designed for a particular problem in a particular period of life, namely adolescence, and reflects a widespread assumption that after marriage sex was enjoyable and desirable.

Most middle-class girls were able to sublimate their desires through a variety of indirect outlets. The young girl's reading was dominated by romantic stories of love, passion and sex; these topics helped to sublimate sex drives and also to provide a hope for later fulfilment,for the characters in the stories sought and found a grand passion. Sexual impulses could be more directly expressed through flirtation. One of the most common questions raised by young girls in the new magazines concerned flirtation and its propriety. Their letters make it quite clear that flirtation became a major preoccupation and pleasure. Hence they constantly asked advice on how to attract a certain young man's fancy:

126

should they introduce themselves first, how could they get a boy to invite them out, did they need to be chaperoned, and so on.[35] Middle-class girls were no shrinking violets; they became increasingly bold in their contacts with the opposite sex.

This new boldness was most clearly seen in their fashions. The young girl wanted to look as appealing to the opposite sex as possible. She went to great pains to make sure that her figure, her hair, and her complexion were sexually appealing. In the 1870s the attributes of good figure were a well-developed bust, a tapering waist (of eighteen inches) and full rounded hips. A woman who wanted to get the eye of a man would play with her feet (admitting only to exercising to keep her ankles slim). Legs were accentuated. One of the most popular fashions of the mid-century was the crinoline. Because it moved readily with the woman's body, it gave the appearance that she was floating on air, and also allowed her to show off her legs whenever she sat down or climbed stairs. There was the conundrum in 1863 which asked 'why may crinoline be justly regarded as a social invention?' the answer – 'Because it enables us to see more of our friends then we used to.'[36] Fashionable neat little boots were part of this new female fashion fetish. Stockings also became sexier as they approached flesh color and were becoming sheerer.

The official adolescent culture of the middle class – that as preached by school-mistresses and sermons – was no sure preparation for sex in marriage. Some girls would not be able successfully to sublimate their sexual desires for some ten years and then upon taking their marriage vows suddenly fulfill them. But most middle-class adult women made the transition relatively easily, and many continued to show the same enthusiasm for their personal appearances – their figures, hair, clothing – as the young girl did, not just to attract attention but to invite sexual activity from their mates. Women's magazines like the young girls' magazines, continually offered advice on how to stay young and how to remain attractive. As a result Victorian women were the first large consumers of what has since become a major industry – cosmetics. Women wanted their skin soft to the touch, free from blemishes and wrinkles. The Victorian woman was the first modern woman in that she thought that she could remain young and attractive forever. Old age was shunned. This is clear from the hundreds of advertisements for skin restorers, hair dyes, and corsets. For a smooth white complexion there was the New Parisian Vaporizer, or Beethan's Glyceran and Cucumber Lotion, which guaranteed to make one years younger. A typical advertisement for corsets read: 'the Specialité Corset leads the way all the world over to Women's greatest ambition, ' Good Figure.' For those who desired a fuller bust there was Diano, a mysterious treatment that claimed the following: 'WOMEN MADE BEAUTIFUL. Develops the

Bust; fill all hollow places . . . Beautiful women everywhere owe their fame and loveliness to Diano.'

A letter written to *The Female Friend* in 1851 by a woman married sixteen years described the growing impulse in this period. She wrote that in addition to the importance of taking care of her home and children, she is extremely particular about her person. A woman who will dress nicely, keep her hair, as long as she can do so, beautiful by washing, oiling and dying, who will make her skin softer, her complexion fresher, her teeth whiter, and who not only bathes daily but sweeten herself by perfume, will please her husband and retain to the last his feeling of love and admiration.[37]

The concern for maintaining an alluring appearance was thus no superficial matter. It served as the basis for an increasing array of cosmetic products. The novelty of the concern did not pass unnoticed, and this was one of the many aspects of women's behavior that drew vigorous criticism. One of the more popular critics was the eccentric Eliza Lynn Linton, author of the notorious work *The Girl of the Period*. The 'Girl of the Period' was 'A creature who dies her hair, paints her face as first articles of her personal religion, a creature whose sole idea of life is fun.'[38] She is bold in her manner. She laughs and flirts with men. In other words the goal of middle-class appearance had become modern, as the desire to remain sexually appealing well after the years of flirtation and courtship took increasingly firm root.

The reason the mature Victorian woman places so much emphasis on her physical appearance is because she expected far more from marriage than had her grandmother fifty years earlier. The Victorian woman married above all for a love relationship. Though traditionalists still urged that the prime purpose of marriage should be procreation of children, this was not the major concern of the middle-class woman. And here we return directly to the question of birth control, the motivations behind it, and the methods used to effect it. With the image of the passionless Victorian woman, it would be easy to conclude, with those few historians who have discussed women at all, that abstinence and *coitus interruptus* were the only means employed by middle-class families once they launched the historic process. Since the passionless woman found intercourse so repulsive anyway, neither of these methods would seem strange; while abstinence might be preferable, *coitus interruptus* might give the woman the satisfaction of doing her duty to her husband without pleasure on either side. However, given that Victorian women were not sexless this whole problem requires a new look.

Certainly the evidence from the marriage manuals casts serious doubt on the idea that abstinence and *coitus interruptus* were effective means of birth control in the nineteenth century.[39] Abstinence was considered harmful and unnatural, even for women. Carlile noted that 'They . . . who abstain from sexual intercourse, are generally useless for the purpose of civil life. They seldom possess either the common cheerfulness or the gaiety of well-supported animal life.' On the effect of abstinence on women he remarked that

It is a fact that can hardly have escaped the notice of anyone, when women who have never had sexual commerce begin to droop when about 25 years of age, that they become pale and languid, that general weakness and irritability, a sort of restlessness, nervous fidgetiness takes possession of them, and an absorbing process goes on, their forms degenerate, their features sink and the peculiar character of the old maid becomes apparent.[40]

This should not be taken to mean that Victorianism should be turned on its head, to reveal eager sexuality.[41] British authorities did warn against excessive sexual intercourse, but their remedy was moderation, not abstinence.[42] For the most part the discussion of sexual excess focused on masturbation, not sex in marriage. By the same token medical authorities objected to *coitus interruptus*. This was considered highly unreliable and detrimental to the nervous system.[43]

Thus we emerge with the following picture, granting again that we lack specific proof on the frequency of use of any birth control method. Middle-class birth control begins toward the mid-nineteenth century. Abstinence and *coitus interruptus* had been known long before the nineteenth century. Both were criticized by virtually all authorities during the century, in terms of desirable sexual pleasure as well as health. There is really no reason to believe that these two methods became suddenly more popular, especially in view of the fact that there were newer and less disruptive methods of birth control available to the Victorians. Many of these methods became known shortly before the middle class began to limit births. Surely, even without conclusive proof, the association is so probable as to merit extensive discussion in interpreting the birth rate decline.

Abortion, unfortunately, remains an unknown quantity. It has been noted that the number of abortions increased in the second half of the century, though of course the relevance of this to the middle class is uncertain.[44] Several spermicides were available early in the century, including 'Female Pills' of various kinds which were supposed to promote an abortion rather than being used as a contraceptive.[45] Among the various abortifacients was Dialehyn pills, which contained lead and hicra-picra (also called hickery-pickery, which was a purgative composed of aloes and canella bark). Judging from the repeated warnings found in the health manuals against inducing miscarriage, it seems possible that some women did resort to this method of birth control; for example, Dr. Edward Tilt noted that

> There are many young married ladies, who not knowing
> how, childlike, to repose in the wisdom of Providence, dread
> having children. They are fearful of being subjected to pain,
> encumbrance and expense, and whenever the monthly flow
> does not appear at the appointed time they take exercise
> in the endeavor to bring it on.[46]

However, it seems very improbable that this method of birth control
was largely employed by middle-class women because it was not
effective and was very painful and dangerous. Abortions were probably
attempted as the last resort to birth control, when some other method
failed.

Another method of birth control that was not new but was given
fuller consideration in the nineteenth century was the concept of the
'safe period' or 'sterile period.' This method certainly could not have
accounted for a significant decline in the birth rate because the 'safe
period' was not safe. There were many contradictory opinions as to the
time of the 'safe period.' Several sources recommended 'the avoidance
of connection, from two days before, till eight days after the monthly
course — at which time impregnation is far most likely to occur.'[47]
Dr. Conquest objected to this idea. He noted that

> It is almost universal opinion that women conceive most
> readily after the periodical discharge ceases, but I do not
> think so; and the result of my inquiry and observation is,
> that women most frequently conceive about fourteen or
> sixteen days after the cessation of the secretion. . .[48]

However, his very apt observation was not generally accepted. As late as
the 1880s, the 'safe period' was still based on the opinion that conception
occurred 'from three days before the monthly flow till eight days after
it.'[49] This serves as another example of the ignorance of the female
system which was so apparent in the earlier discussion of gynecology.
It is doubtful that many middle-class women relied upon this very
uncertain means of birth control, if they were successfully bent on
limiting their family size.

Thus we are left with one final means of birth control to examine —
contraception. The development of contraceptive devices in the
nineteenth century has been noted as a 'Vital revolution' [50] and
constitutes the key to the decline in the birth rate. The nineteenth
century witnessed for the first time the mass production and mass
advertising of contraceptive devices. The most striking feature in the
development of contraceptive techniques, which has never been
adequately pursued, was its impact on women. For one of the
distinguishing features of nineteenth-century contraceptives was that
they placed control in the hands of the women. Also, the propaganda

for the use of these devices was directed particularly at the woman, for all were hailed as contributing significantly to the health and happiness of the woman. It has often been noted that birth control was basic to any emancipation of women;[51] we can now see that middle-class women, their concept of self-interest already changing, chose many of the methods by which the emancipation was effected.

One of the first breakthroughs for the woman was in the development of the sponge as a contraceptive. Here for the first time the woman was given the means to control her own body. The role of Francis Place and Richard Carlile in making known this method of contraception has been duly recognized,[52] but its significance for the Victorian woman has not been followed up. The sponge was first introduced to England in 1823 by Place in his notorious 'Diabolical Handbills.' Since Place has been associated traditionally with the radical cause and working classes, his birth control message has been somewhat underrated, being viewed as being primarily limited to the working classes. And since there was no visible decline in birth rates among this sector of society until late in the century, the contribution has been considered minimal. However, Place had much broader appeal. It seems more probable to suppose that the middle class was reading Place's work than that the working class took it up widely in view of the level of literacy at this point. Though Place's appeal for birth control was essentially economic and one of his handbills was written directly to the working class, he also wrote a handbill specifically for the middle class, in which he emphasized strongly the health of women. In the pamphlet entitled *To The Married of Both Sexes in Genteel Life*, Place made the following case for women and birth control:

> Among the many sufferings of married women as mothers, there are two cases, which command the utmost sympathy and commiseration. The first arises from constitutional peculiarities, or weaknesses. The second from malconformation of the bones of the Pelvis. The first named case produces miscarriages, and brings on the state of existence scarcely endurable. It has caused thousands of respectable women to linger on in pain and apprehension, till at length, death has put an end to the almost inconceivable suffering. The second case is always attended with immediate risk of life. Pregnancy never terminates without intense suffering, seldom without the death of the child, frequently with the death of the mother, and sometimes with the death of both mother and child.[53]

Richard Carlile's recommendation for the adoption of birth control by the woman was far more positive, as was suggested above in his discussion of female sexuality. However, the full significance of Carlile's

Every Woman's Book has been obscured for the same reasons Place's work was. Carlile's struggle for the free press and his association with the radicals has caused his work on birth control to be considered as destined solely for the working class, which was not the case. Carlile's book sold over 10,000 copies in two years,[54] which indicates that there was widespread interest in this type of information as early as the 1820s. As Carlile's title indicates, the appeal for birth control was made specifically to women. In the Preface, he wrote that

> The modest and chaste woman may be assured that nothing is here meant to offend her. Instruction, upon a matter, of which both men and women are by far too ignorant, for their welfare and happiness, is the sole object of this publication. It may shock prejudices, but it will be approved by reason and due deliberation.[55]

Carlile emphasized the need for birth control solely for the benefits it offered the woman. His philosophy was that birth control was 'the very bulwark of love, the promoter of wisdom, of beauty, of health and happiness.'[56] With birth control women would be able to enjoy sex more, since the fear of conception would be removed.[57] Carlile noted that with birth control 'Women, if we may be allowed the expression, would be in much greater demand, as every young man would take a wife and women would be all but infinitely more respected than they are now.'[58]

Carlile recommended several birth control methods, including the condom and *coitus interruptus*. However, the best plan was the sponge because it placed control in the hands of the woman and was far more reliable. Carlile gave the following directions for the use of the sponge:

> . . . before sexual intercourse, the female introduces into her vagina a piece of sponge, as large as can be pleasantly introduced, having previously attached a bobbin or bit of narrow riband to withdraw it, it will be found a prevention to conception, while it neither lessens the pleasure of the female nor injures her health.[59]

He went on to explain its benefits;

> . . . the writer has been informed by those who have made experiments upon the matter, that the sponge is not felt by either party during coition, and that no portion of pleasure is abated; while on the other hand, the pleasure is increased in the removal of all dread of evil consequences.[60]

The popularity of the works of Place and Carlile, plus the very significant fact that the sponge remained one of the most highly recommended means of birth control throughout the nineteenth century, demonstrates that women did play a vital role not only in the decision to limit the number of births but also in its implementation.

132

The second important advance in the field of birth control for women was the syringe. This means of contraception was first introduced in England in 1834, with the publication of Charles Knowlton's *Fruits of Philosophy*.[61] The benefits of the syringe, as noted by Knowlton, were that it was cheap, harmless, would not cause sterility, involved no sacrifice during coitus, and most important of all, placed control in the hands of the woman where it ought to be.[62]

The Knowlton syringe was a soft metal barrel and a piston head tightened with a wrapping of tow. Knowlton was not very precise about the strength of the solutions, and suggested that the woman make it as strong as she could tolerate. He did, however, give the following recommendations on various types of solutions to be used:

1. Of Alum, to a pint of water, a lump as large as a large chestnut.
2. Of Sulphate of Zinc, to a pint of water, a large thimble full.
3. Of Sal Eratus, to a pint of water, two common sized *even* teaspoons full.
4. Of good Vinegar, to a pint of water, four or five greatspoons full.
5. Liquid Chloride of Soda, to a pint of water, four or five greatspoons full.

Also a dash of 'spirits' should be added to the solution to keep it from freezing. When the above ingredients were not available, Knowlton quite confidently asserted that 'a liberal use of pretty cold water would be a never-failing preventative.'[63] He advised the woman to douche two or three times freely within five minutes of coitus.[64]

Another important advance in contraceptive techniques which significantly altered the role of woman was the vaginal diaphragm, which covered a wide variety of pessaries. It was previously noted that there were over one hundred different types of pessaries developed; that they were not used exclusively for uterine disorders is quite clear. Dr. Routh implied this in the following comment:

In a debate before the Medical Society of London, on the use of the intra-uterine stem, devised originally for uterine disorders, we were credibly informed that they were also used by some ladies of high position and continually worn by them with a view to prevent conception.[65]

It is not known for certain when the vaginal diaphragm, or cervical cap, was first introduced in England. However, it seems fairly well accepted that with the vulcanization of rubber in 1843, the cervical cap was made extremely popular because it was now softer and therefore more comfortable to use; it was also more durable and cheaper.[66]

Thus by 1850, the woman had three fairly effective means of birth control available to her: the sponge (1823), the douche (1834), and the diaphragm (1840s). All three methods remained widely recommended procedures and were vastly improved upon within the century. One of the first improvements in using the sponge resulted from the recommendation that it be used in combination with a douche. This was advised as a most effective means of contraception by George Drysdale in his popular work, *Elements of Social Science,*[67] which was first published in 1854 and went through thirty-five editions and sold 80,000 copies by the end of the century. It was also suggested that the sponge first be soaked in a quinine solution.[68] Later in the century there was the artificial sponge or vaginal tampon which contained in its center a friable capsule filled with a quinine solution. 'All the woman would have to do before intercourse would be to take one of the tampons, and squeeze it, which would break the capsule, setting free the solution which would then permeate the whole sponge. She would then insert it into the vagina as far as possible.'[69]

As with the sponge, there were improvements with the syringe. One of the advancements on the Knowlton syringe was the Vertical and Reverse Current Syringe. The following advertisement for this device explained its utility:

> The improved appliance is . . . A New Vertical and Reverse Current Vaginal Tube, producing a continual current treble the power of the ordinary tubes used for this purpose, thoroughly cleansing the parts it is applied to. It is to be used with injection of sufficient power to destroy the life properties of the spermatic fluid without injury to the person, and if the instructions are followed it can be used with success and safety.[70]

The 'Irrigator' was another improvement on the syringe. It was claimed to be superior to the traditional syringe because it did not require the woman to leave the bed, thus avoiding the damage of catching a chill. But it did require extensive preparation and some dexterity on the part of the woman. The Irrigator was a can holding about two pints which was hung against the wall by the woman's side of the bed, at a height of some four feet or more above the level of her head. Before getting into bed the woman was to fill the can with a solution of alum, or quinine, and place a bed pan and towel on a chair at the side of her bed. After connection all the woman had to do was turn her back and slip the bedpan under her, then inject the mouth-piece of the tube into the vagina, as far as possible, and turn the tap; the solution flowed in and out without causing wetting or trouble, or so the recommendation said.[71] No doubt the sponge and the simple syringe remained most popular but the very fact that these elaborate devices were known and sold shows that women were indeed willing to go to considerable lengths to prevent pregnancy.

The rubber pessary was also constantly being improved. One of the more commonly referred to pessaries was the Check Pessary. An advertisement for it listed the following benefits:

> The improved Check Pessary is a simply devised instrument of pure soft medicated rubber to be worn by the female during (coition) as a protection against conception. It is constructed on a common-sense principle and strictly in accordance with the female organization; can be worn any length of time with ease and comfort; does not interfere in any way with coition (intercourse) and so accurately fits the parts that it adapts itself perfectly, and no apprehension of it going too far need be felt and with care will last for years. The improved *Check Pessary* is largely recommended by medical men . . . as it is a perfect, convenient and safe protection against conception and pregnancy, and the only article of the kind that can be used without the inconvenience or knowledge of the husband.[72]

Dr. Allbutt, in *The Wife's Handbook*, gave the following description of a preventive pessary:

> The pessary is in shape something like a round dishcover, the dome portion of which is made of thin, smooth india-rubber which will collapse with a touch. The rim surrounding the cover portion is made of a ring of thick rubber which can be squeezed to any shape. The hollow portion of the pessary is intended to cover the neck and mouth of the womb during intercourse, so that no semen may penetrate into the womb.[73]

He recommended as an additional precaution when using the pessary that 'Before removing the pessary in the morning, the woman would do wisely to syringe the vagina with tepid water – or with alum and water; or better still, with a weak quinine solution.[74] In the 1880s there were quinine pessaries made of cocoa-butter and quinine which dissolved when placed in the vagina, allowing the quinine to escape and destroy the activity of the sperm.[75]

It is impossible to date exactly the developments in the improved birth control techniques, and as opposed to the earlier introduction of the basic new devices. However, by the early 1880s they were beginning to be advertised in the women's magazines and health manuals. Indeed the advertisements of the '80s reflect the fact that these methods were well-known and widely used because their emphasis was typically on the improvements made in existing devices. By the end of the century there was an endless variety of contraceptive devices for women, indicating the continuing demand. The following list indicated the extensive improvements made on the original three methods:

The Rendell Pessary – soluble quinine pessary at 2s. per doz.

The Improved Prolapsus Check Pessaries – 3 sizes – 2s.3d. ea.

Messinga Pessary with Spring Rim – 3 sizes – 3s. each

The Gem Pessary with Sponge Dome – 5s. each

The Spring Unique Pessary with Solid or Inflated Rim 1s.6d; 3s.6d. each

Inflated Ball Pessary – 3 sizes – 3s.6d. each

Contraceptive Sponge – enclosed in a silk net – 1s. each

Quinine Compound – 1s; 2s. per box

Vulcanite Syringe – 3s.6d. each

Vertical and Reverse Syringe – 5s.6d. each[76]

Before concluding on the subject of birth control, mention must be made of the condom which, although not new, remained a very popular and often recommended means of contraception in the nineteenth century, especially after vulcanization of rubber made it more durable and less expensive. Even though the condom is viewed as a male contraceptive, the role of the woman in its use was at the very least co-operative. An article written in 1844 on the benefits of the 'nightcap' or condom over other contraceptive devices went to great lengths to illustrate the benefits to the woman's health and pleasure in the use of this technique.[77] The author objected to the syringe because it involved a great deal of inconvenience both before and after intercourse for the woman. He observed that one problem with douching before was that

... if, when alum is used, the husband allows himself too much time for preliminary fondling previous to entering the *sanctum sanctorum*, he will find it harsh to the sensation of contact; and, indeed, partially impracticable, until some very vigorous efforts be used. The lady will at the same time, suffer from the rudeness of the friction.[78]

He noted also several objections to the sponge. He cautioned that the sponge

... *must not be too large.* A piece which, when extended with water, is about the size of the glandular extremity of the gentleman's penis, is quite large enough, if it be greater dimension it will not remain at the remote end of the cell even when placed there; and if the gentleman's machine be of respectable length, it is liable to push the sponge on one side, and some of the seed will be deposited at the very door of the womb. The string also is frequently found to be in the very midst of the channel, and however paradoxical it may seem, it is strictly true, that this plan sometimes obliges both male and female to pursure their pleasure with an

accompaniment of the most lively symptoms of pain. Under
such circumstances the sponge is liable to be pulled out by
mutual consent, exactly at the time when it most requisite
that it should be kept in.[79]

The need for co-operation between the male and the female in the use
of the condom was very explicitly stated in the description of the
method of procedure:

No interference with the usual course of proceedings is
necessary until the last few moments of bliss. The conjugal
endearments may even proceed to actual possession and
enjoyment, but when nature warns the gentleman that his
satisfaction is about to be completed by the stupendous
effort of the vital stream, he warns the lady, who having
previously to yielding herself to his arms, softened a nightcap
in warm water, snatches it from her pillow, and with her
two thumbs and forefingers draws it over the burning
machine, which may then be instantly replaced in its natural
receptable for the fruition of mutual love, the entire
interruption not occupying more than 5 or 6 seconds.[80]

The author went on to emphasize the benefits of this method for the
woman.

Ladies will absolutely suffer no inconvenience from it. The
cap will not disturb their complete satisfaction in the least.
Are not the smiles of an affectionate wife abundant
repayment for a very slight restraint?[81]

Finally, the same essay harshly critisized the husband who did not
protect his wife by using the condom:

See your pale and emaciated female, surrounded by
consumptive children. Is it not horrible that she should be
bearing also an unborn babe to add to their number?
What a brute and slaughtering foe to her is her 'husband,'
if he be aware that a prudential check exists to prevent such
a birth as awaits him, and such a death as his unchecked
passion hastens to his wife.[82]

Thus it can be suggested that even with the condom, which was not
directly in her control, the woman still maintained an important role.
Here, too, woman's health and pleasure were important considerations
in the decision to limit the number of births.

Nevertheless, it is probable that the most significant devices involved
in the middle-class birth rate decline were the sponge, the douche, and
the vaginal diaphragm. One cannot ignore the fact that all the other
methods — abstinence, *coitus interruptus*, and the condom — were
well-known before the nineteenth century, yet it was not until the
introduction and development of the three new methods of birth

control that the birth rate began to drop significantly. The fact that the newer methods were designed for the female at a time when she was beginning to exert more and more control over her body also cannot be ignored. Just as the woman rejected the fatalistic attitude related to pain in childbirth and sought chloroform, just as she rejected the fatalistic attitude toward the discomfort and burden of nursing and sought artificial feeding methods, so she rejected the fatalistic attitude to the inevitability of pregnancy and sought contraceptive devices. Is it mere coincidence that as the burdens and responsibilities of motherhood increased the demand for and production of birth control methods particularly for the woman also increased? Overall, the array of available contraceptive devices makes it abundantly clear that the woman was an important factor in the decision-making process. This is not to imply that the husband had no part to play, though the advertisement for the Check Pessary suggested that this might sometimes be the case. The mutuality of decision-making so commonly invoked by the marriage manuals may well have operated in this area. We can reasonably be sure that the woman was no passive partner and that her changing values and situation — even more than economic factors — heavily influenced the decision taken, whether by husband and wife together or, as was technically possible, by the wife alone.

The Victorian middle-class women experienced dramatic changes in her role as mother. She challenged the traditional attitude toward infant mortality and maternal mortality by seeking advice on better care for herself and the child. Unfortunately, until very late in the nineteenth century, the challenge was successful only in so far as she was able to limit the number of children she had, and thereby lessen the risk of death for herself and her child. Here again, the development of birth control is a vital feature of the history of Victorian motherhood.

The Victorian woman took her role as mother seriously. She realized the importance of the new emphasis on the intimate relationship of mother to child, which added significantly not only to the physical work involved with child care, but also to the mental strain on the mother's part. She assumed complete responsibility for the future health and happiness of her child. The new birth control methods aided her in meeting her responsibilities as mother and helped eliminate an important threat to her life and health.

Notes

1. John W. Innes, *Class Fertility Trends in England and Wales 1876-1934* (Princeton, 1938), p. 1.
2. Ibid., pp. 1-11.
3. Norman E. Himes, *Medical History of Contraception* (New York, 1936), pp. 239-40.

138

4. A. Newsholme and T.H.C. Stevenson, 'The Decline of Human Fertility in the United Kingdom and Other Countries as shown by Corrected Birth Rates,' in the *Journal of the Royal Statistical Society*, Volume LXIX (1906), Part. I.
5. Himes, *Medical History*, p. 397.
6. *Report of the Royal Commission on Population*, Vol. XIX (1948-9).
7. As discussed in Banks' *Prosperity and Parenthood*, p.6.
8. Ibid., p. 167.
9. See Ch. 1, note 13.
10. Banks' Prosperity and Parenthood pp. 167-8.
11. Charles Morazé *La France Bourgeoise* (Paris, 1952).
12. Full reference is cited in Note. 1.
13. Innes, *Class Fertility Trends*, pp. 58-9.
14. As against the strange argument in Edward Shorter, 'Female Emancipation, Birth Control, and Fertility in European History,' *American Historical Review*, Vol. 98, No. 3 (June 1973), which admits the vital role of birth control in women's modernization, but sees it initially as a defensive, fearful measure.
15. Alan Armstrong, in his study *Stability and Change*, noted that middle-class families were practising birth control as early as the 1840s (p. 173).
16. Richard Carlile, *Every Woman's Book; or What is Love* (London, 1836), pp. 36-7.
17. *Beauty is Power* (London, 1871), p. 177.
18. Dr. Elizabeth Blackwell, *How to Keep a Household in Health* (London, 1870), p. 8.
19. Austin Holyoake, *Large or Small Families? On Which Side Lies the Balance of Comfort?* (London, 1870), p. 5.
20. *The Family Economist*, Vol. I (1848), p. 44.
21. *The English Matron*, p. 17.
22. Ryan, *The Philosophy of Marriage*, pp. 114-5.
23. William Acton, *The Functions and Disorders of the Reproductive Organs in Childhood, Youth, Adult Age, and Advanced Life, Considered in Their Physiological, Social and Moral Relations* (London, 1862).
24. McGregor, *Divorce in England*: Peter T. Cominos, 'Innocent Femina Sensualis in Unconscious Conflict,' in Vicinus (ed.), *Suffer and Be Still*: Crow, *The Victorian Woman.*
25. Acton, *The Functions of the Reproductive Organs*, p. 112.
26. *The London Medical Review*, Vol. III, No. 111 (September 1862), p. 145. Even conservative observers were aware of female sensuality as indicated from the following remarks of a correspondent to *The Times* (4 Nov. 1847): 'One would really think to listen to some sentimentalists, that man alone derived any sensual gratification from these indulgences and that there were no animal passion in woman to tempt her in the same direction. Women yield not to the solicitation of men, but to the solicitations of their own impure desires.'
27. Carlile, *Every Woman's Book*, p. 8.
28. Ibid., p. 14.
29. Dr. Elizabeth Blackwell, *The Human Element in Sex: Being a Medical Enquiry into the Relationship of Sexual Physiology to Christian Morality*, 2nd ed. (London, 1885).
30. Dr. Elizabeth Blackwell, *Counsel to Parents on the Moral Education of Their Children* (London 1878).
31. Ryan, *The Philosophy of Marriage*, p. 114-5.
32. Allbutt, *The Wife's Handbook*, p. 57.
33. The age of puberty has been falling on an average of three to four months per decade for the last 125 years. There is evidence that the onset of puberty is

class-specific. In a study of women in Manchester in 1820 it was found that the age of menarche among working women was 15.7 compare to 14.6 for girls of the middle class. (J.M. Tanner, 'The Trend Toward Earlier Physical Maturation,' in J.E. Meade and A.S. Parkes (eds.), *Biological Aspects of Social Problems* (New York, 1965), p. 51.

One of the factors accounting for this decline in puberty and its class distinctions relates to nutritional levels: the higher the nutritional level the lower the age of menarche. Recent medical research suggests that the onset of puberty is related to a girl's critical weight — 47 kilograms. The age at which this weight is attained is probably related to food consumption and social class. See R.E.F. Frisch, 'Critical Weight and Menarche, Initiation of the Adolescent Growth Spirit and Control of Puberty,' in Melvin Grumbach (ed.), *Control of the Onset of Puberty* (New York, 1974), pp. 403-23. Along with the nutritional factor should be added the psychological element. The increased sexual stimuli found in the urban environment has also been related to a decline in the onset of puberty. Flirtation and courtship patterns made these stimuli fully relevant to middle-class girls, perhaps even disproportionately so, contrary to the impressions of class prudery, while many working-class girls, more isolated as servants, experienced a smaller range of stimulating contacts.

34. Allbutt, *The Wife's Handbook*, p. 53.
35. The *EDM* was often filled with such queries, see Vol. VII, No. 44, p. 96.
36. Crow, *The Victorian Woman*, p. 123.
37. *The Female Friend*, Vol. 4 (1851), p. 11.
38. E. Lynn Linton, *The Girl of the Period*, Vol. 1, p.2.
39. The only popular manual to recommend abstinence as the best means of birth control was Robert Dale Owen, *Moral Physiology, or a Brief and Plain Treatise on the Population Question* (New York, 1831).
40. Carlile, *Every Woman's Book*, p. 35.
41. Other recent studies indicate similar revisionist interpretation as they recognize that the advice in the manual literature was far from unanimous in condemnation of sex, and that behavior could have departed from conservative forebodings in any event. Indeed the very proliferation of the conservative manuals might suggest a reaction to changing behavior. See the works of Robert V. Wells, 'Family History and Demographic Transition,' *Journal of Social History*, Vol. 9, No. 1 (September 1975), and R.P. Neuman, 'Masturbation, Madness and the Modern Concepts of Childhood and Adolescence,' *Journal of Social History*, Vol. 8, No 3 (March 1975), and Carl. N. Degler, 'What Ought to be and What Was: Women's Sexuality in the Nineteenth Century, *'American Historical Review*,' Vol. 79, No. 5 (December 1974), pp. 1467-90.

One other point must be made about a subject that at the least should be seriously reconsidered. If the host of advocates of unusual middle-class Victorian prudery are correct they must account for, as they have not heretofore, an additional empirical problem. We know that in the twentieth century middle-class sexual behavior is imaginative and active when measured for example by working-class norms; see Les Rainwater *et. al., Workingman's Wife: Her Personality, World and Life Style* (New York, 1959). This implies a major overturning of past middle-class sexual values that has never been identified chronologically, much less explained. Given the new evidence available for the nineteenth century, it seems more probable, as well as more economical, to argue that twentieth-century behavior is an outgrowth of the nineteenth century rather than a complete revolution.

42. Moderation was recommended in Allbutt's *The Wife's Handbook*, p. 7, and in

the review article of Acton's book in *The London Medical Review*, Vol. III (September 1862), p. 145.

43. (George Drysdale), *The Elements of Social Science; or Physical, Sexual and Natural Religion, An Exposition of the True Cause and Only Cure of the Three Primary Social Evils: Poverty, Prostitution, and Celibacy, By a Doctor of Medicine* (London, 1854), p. 359; Allbutt, *The Wife's Handbook*, p. 47.

44. Banks, *Prosperity and Parenthood*, p. 142

45. Clive Wood and Beryl Suitters, *The Fight for Acceptance: A History of Contraception* (Aylesbury, 1970), p. 12.

46. Tilt, *Elements of Health*, p. 261; also found in Bull, *Hints to Mothers*, pp. 103-4, and Conquest, *Letters to a Mother*, p. 6.

47. Charles Knowlton, *Fruits of Philosophy; or The Private Companion of young married couples* (London, 1833?), p. 16; also found in Mason, *The Philosophy of Female Health*, p. 7.

48. Conquest, *Letters to a Mother*, p. 18.

49. Allbutt, *The Wife's Handbook*, p. 47.

50. Himes, *Medical History of Contraception*, p. 391.

51. For a recent and quite persuasive discussion of the subject see Edward Shorter, 'Female Emancipation,' pp. 605-40.

52. Peter Fryer, *The Birth Controllers* (London 1965), and Himes, *Medical History of Contraception*.

53. Francis Place, *To the Married of Both Sexes in Genteel Life* (1823), Place Collection, British Museum, Vol. IXI, Pt. II, p. 43.

54. Carlile made this claim in the Preface to the 1828 edition.

55. Carlile, *Every Woman's Book*, Preface.

56. Ibid., p. 25.

57. Ibid., p. 23.

58. Ibid., p. 36.

59. Ibid., p. 38.

60. Ibid., p. 39.

61. Full reference was given in Note. 37.

62. Himes, *Medical History of Contraception*, p. 228.

63. Shirley Green, *The Curious History of Contraception* (London 1971), p. 67.

64. Himes, *Medical History of Contraception*, p. 228.

65. Wood and Suiters, *The Fight For Acceptance*, p. 107.

66. Ibid., p. 29; Himes, *Medical History of Contraceptives*.

67. Full reference was given in Note 33.

68. Allbutt, *The Wife's Handbook*, p. 48.

69. Ibid., p. 49.

70. Ibid., advertisement.

71. Ibid., pp. 47-8.

72. Ibid., advertisement.

73. Ibid., pp. 48-9.

74. Ibid., p. 49.

75. Ibid., p. 49.

76. John Peel, 'The Manufacture and Retailing of Contraceptives in England,' in *Population Studies*, Vol. 17 (1963), p. 110.

77. 'On the Use of Night-Caps – Seven Years Experience of the Practicability of Limiting the Number of a Family, by the Best Known Methods; Including some Valuable and Novel Information, Never Before Published; Addressed Exclusively to Married Couples by a Married Man (with six children)' (1844), quoted in Peter Fryer, *The Man of Pleasure's Companion; a Nineteenth*

141

Century Anthology of Amorous Entertainment (London, 1965).

78. Ibid., p. 122.
79. Ibid., p. 123.
80. Ibid., p. 128.
81. Ibid., p. 128.
82. Ibid., p. 124

PART III

CONCLUSIONS

8 MIDDLE-CLASS WOMEN AND MODERNIZATION

After an examination of some of the more important aspects in the life
of the middle-class woman, one begins seriously to question if the
Victorian woman, as she has so long been depicted, ever really existed.
Certainly, the woman whose life was characterized as leisurely,
dependent, prudish, and boring was not the married middle-class
woman of the nineteenth century. Whether or not the image applies to
upper-class women remains to be investigated, and it is a task worth
undertaking in nineteenth-century English social history. The woman
portrayed in this study perhaps lacked some of the glamor and romantic
flavor of the woman in the image. However her life, viewed in terms of
realities, in terms of the problems she encountered, gives the Victorian
woman more meaning and substances than ever before. Within the
context of the family, her role was not only functional but central and
crucial. One could not possibly understand anything about the
Victorian family without understanding the woman in the family, who
nurtured it, who managed it, who comforted it. In her role as mistress
of the house, in her relationship with domestics and most importantly,
in her role as mother, the middle-class woman of the nineteenth century
defined herself.

Yet the middle-class woman's historical role transcended the
boundaries of the family during the nineteenth century, for she was
caught up in the broader transformation of English society. In her
daily functions she began to develop attitudes and behavior patterns
that form part of the process of modernization. The evolution was
incomplete, even well after the 1880s, for the middle-class woman
retained important links with traditional values. And assessment in
these terms is complicated by the failure, heretofore, to apply any
but economic criteria of modernization to the history of women.[1]
Nevertheless, the stresses and problems with which this study
has been concerned cannot be understood without relating them to a
more fundamental evolution, in which middle-class women led the way.
If other women, many of them unmarried, seem as individuals closer to
a modern set of values during the nineteenth century, the married
middle-class women constituted the first large category to undergo the
modernization process, precisely because they applied it within the
context of the family.

Before proceeding with this discussion, it is necessary to elaborate
the precise definition of modernization. Modernization involves
industrialization and urbanization on a broad scale. Concentrated
population centers replace isolated rural communities as the normal

144

human environment. The nature of work obviously changes, and the bulk of the populace is removed from the land. And modernization brings about not only changes in work and style of living, but also a new attitude of mind, which in the long run is probably its more significant feature.

Modern man has conventionally been defined as possessing a mentality that, for the most part, is open to innovation and new experiences. This involves belief in planning and organization in every aspect of life, in the benefits of science and technology, and a conviction that one's environment was calculable, that it could be improved. The modern mind rejects fatalism, and it is present- and future-oriented rather than backward-looking.[2] Characterization of modern man in many ways defines the new middle-class man of the nineteenth century, and in combination the modernization theme and progressive middle-class values are familiar enough. But what about modern woman? Since this study claimed from the outset that the Victorian middle-class woman was the first modern woman, it is necessary to apply the definition of modernization to her life. Did she follow the same pattern? Did she share the same outlook?

The process of modernization was never a voluntary process for women (nor was it for men). It was more a result of outside forces, the new pressures of urban industrial society coming together and making their impact in the nineteenth century, first on the values of the middle class. More than her upper-class sister or her working-class sister, the middle-class woman, in order to maintain herself in this period of great transition, had to adapt to new economic means and a new environment. The working- and upper-class woman long maintained more traditional life styles. For example, the upper-class woman never encountered the economic pressures which continually perplexed the middle-class woman in her effort to maintain an appropriate living standard. The upper-class woman could still afford her retinue of servants and enjoy the society and seasons of the fashionable world during most of the nineteenth century. While the working-class woman shared more of the experiences of the middle-class woman, on the whole, and was certainly deeply affected by industrialization, her life was restricted by a number of factors. Her material means were long insufficient to enable her to alter greatly her lot in life. Her education and outlook were not the same as that of the middle-class woman. Her attitudes toward ordering her home and children remained tradition-bound for the greater part of the nineteenth century. In some respects, in the initial reaction to industrialization the working-class woman developed a special function in preserving as many traditional familial values as possible, to cushion the shock of change.[3] In contrast, the middle-class woman was ultimately able not only to react to change but

145

to initiate some changes on her own. The primary impulse toward modernization stemmed from the middle-class woman's accession to a modest level of prosperity which ultimately brought about a new life style — a lifestyle defined by middle-class values and goals — which neither imitated the aristocracy or attempted to throw up purely traditional defenses against change within the family.

The impact of urban living was profound for the middle-class woman of the nineteenth century. The problems of urbanization — overcrowding, polluted waters and air — were not of great concern for upper-class woman, who maintained control of the better sections of the city during most of the century. Also the upper-class woman was able to maintain her traditional rural ties by keeping a place in the country. However, urban society was the only life for the new middle-class woman and in this she shared many of the problems of urbanization with the working-class woman. But in contrast to the ability of many working-class wives to recreate a supportive family network,[4] the middle-class woman was more on her own. Admittedly, until a serious investigation is made into the demographic changes of the middle class in the nineteenth century, we have to rely upon impressionistic evidence. It appears from the literature of the day that one of the special problems for the middle-class woman was the frequent changing of residence.[5] The results of this constant state of flux was that the middle-class woman had no sense of roots, no sense of belonging to an established community, and often lacked strong extended family ties. It is interesting to note that in all the various sources used for this study, there is no mention of any type of family relationship beyond the nuclear family. Never once was there a reference to the role of grandparents, aunts, uncles, or cousins. This lack of relationships beyond the immediate family was particularly striking in the discussions on pregnancy. It would seem likely that at this very important event in a woman's life she would have her mother or sister or some other close relative assist her. However, the middle-class woman was advised to seek the aid of a friendly neighbor. The absence of guidance from experienced kin could have accounted for the middle-class woman's need for such fundamental advice on child care. Also the middle-class woman would be able to innovate in child-rearing more easily without the more tradition-bound influence of her mother. She was certainly freer to adopt artificial feeding methods and contraceptive techniques.

Another important aspect of the modernization process in the lives of married middle-class woman, which must be viewed as both cause and result, was the declining influence of religion in their lives. Historians have generally accepted and documented the overall decline of religion in the nineteenth century. It is well known that the returns of the Religious Census of 1851 indicated severe limitations in the numbers attending church, for approximately half the population was not present at religious services. Contemporaries claimed that widespread absenteeism was due mainly to a waning of religion among the working class, and subsequent historians have generally accepted this position.[6] However, more recently, it has been noted that 'there was proportionately as much conscious unbelief, if not indifference, in the Victorian middle-class as amongst the workers . . .'[7] Yet even if this point is accepted it is tempting to assume that indifference was confined to men only; and the image of the Victorian middle-class woman as extremely pious and religious continues to persist. However, there were some indications of changes in women's outlook during the nineteenth century which suggest, at least, a growing modification of traditional religious beliefs. There is no need to claim complete separation or a defined anti-religious sentiment; but religion lost some of its meaning for middle-class women.

One indication of the declining influence of religion was the increasing secularism of the material read by women. In the early years of the century, the printed matter for women was primarily of a religious nature. By the second half of the century, the literature was almost completely lacking in religious inspiration. The few religious magazines, such as *The British Mothers' Magazine,* constantly bemoaned the decline of religion among the fairer sex. One example of the new trend of secularism was found in the editorial policy of the very popular *EDM,* which stated that it was the policy of the magazine to exclude all religious composition from its pages. It would not answer any theological questions, or even publish poetry of a religious nature.[8] Looking through the hundreds of magazines printed in the nineteenth century for women, one is left with the impression that women were more concerned with the condition of their wash or the nature of their complexions than the state of their souls.

In sum, middle-class women shared with other groups many of the general pressures of urbanization. They shared also a decline of religious interest, and this may have had a distinctive impact on them because of their exposure to secular reading materials. Their ability to modernize was particularly enhanced by an unusually nucleated family structure and by the ability to forge a standard of living above the subsistence level. Other causes may have been involved, for we are in a better position to describe the modernization process than to assess the reasons for its special applicability to middle-class women, but even this short list suffices to explain why middle-class women were able to innovate in response to new pressures.

But not all middle-class women could adapt. Even for most, as we shall see, modernization should not be regarded as a triumphant conquest of progress over tradition but as a painful, often confusing, reaction to change. Some women could not manage even this, especially given the real physical burdens that still defined their lot. As with most social groups, middle-class women divided between adapters and non-adapters, although we are not yet in a position to suggest the size of the latter group and the boundary line is admittedly unclear.

The rapidity and vastness of change could cause a sense of bewilderment, which was especially difficult for many women to cope with because they had very little outlet for their tensions. The growing sense of insecurity seen in the many letters asking for advice is one sign of the tensions modern society produced in the life of the middle-class woman. Forced into the mainstream of a new style of living, the middle-class woman developed anxieties, as we have suggested, in the study of her various roles in the family. The changing concept of motherhood is a case in point. The middle-class woman believed that she could be a better mother so she ventured new methods of child-rearing. However, she was still very insecure about the new ways; hence the continual seeking of advice, perhaps as a source of reassurance. In some respects aspirations changed more rapidly than reality, as in the desire for better health or for an orderly improvement in the standard of living, which added frustrations to anxieties.

Not surprisingly, given the tensions of initial modernization, some symptoms of disturbance emerged among some middle-class women. There is evidence that some women sought refuge in alcohol and drugs. The subject of alcoholism among women was discussed a number of times, indicating that it was a serious problem for some. In 1870, a letter appeared in the *EDM* from 'A Sufferer of Low Spirits,' asking advice from other women on her problem with depression and alcohol.[9] Especially in the health manuals, women were often warned about the ill effects of alcohol. In the manual, *The New Home; Or Wedded Life*, the story was told of a young girl who came to realize the folly of taking a little gin, or brandy, or beer every time she was low, overworked, or simply out of sorts. The relief it offered was very brief, but the destruction it wrought upon her health was lasting.[10] Another indication that women might have resorted to alcohol is suggested by the article, 'Intemperance in Women, with Special Reference to its Effects on the Reproductive System,' which appeared in *The British Medical Journal*. The author noted that one of the principal causes of alcoholism among women was domestic problems.[11]

Drugs were commonly used in the nineteenth century and were readily available, as was seen in the discussion of infant mortality. There is, again, no direct evidence about the use of drugs by women, but some contemporary observers noted a problem here too. For example, Dr. Robert Dick, in his health manual, made the following observation on the need of drugs by women:

> Many women would pass the most indifferent night; many
> would be inadequate to the task or duty of entertaining their
> guests or meeting their friends; in others the chagrins of life
> would prey too severely; regrets and disappointments and
> painful reminiscents would visit them too acutely did they
> not deaden the poignancy of suffering, actual or
> remembered, by the 'drowsy syrups'; . . . or by something
> analogous.[12]

He remarked that many women, because of the pressures of society,
needed artificial sedatives or stimulants, such as opium, morphia,
hyoscyamus, prussic acid, camphor, musk and valerian.[13] Further
indication of the probability of considerable drug use comes in the
many home remedies found in the manuals and periodicals for headaches
or sleeplessness which included strong dosages of drugs. The following
is a preparation recommended for use as a sedative: orange flower
water − 2 oz., laurel water − 1 oz., syrup of poppies − ½ oz., acetate
of morphia − ½ grain. A teaspoon of the above was to be taken every
hour.[14]

All of this, obviously, involves impressionistic evidence. There is no
reason to suggest that alcoholism or abuse of drugs were the normal lot
of middle-class women or even that they necessarily followed from the
tensions of modernization in every case. The extent of the phenomena
cannot presently be determined, but they must be taken into account
both because they suggest an interesting group of women who could not
cope with their lot and because they emphasize some of the pressures
that women more generally encountered during the period.

The more durable impact of modernization on the life of the middle-
class woman can be seen more directly by looking back upon the
discussion of mistress of the house. It was shown that the middle-class
woman's most important considerations here were time and money.
She never seemed to have enough of either, so they required of her
careful planning and organization. Admittedly, she was not totally
successful in meeting these requirements, but she did display a willingness
to accept and try the new concepts. She was the major purchaser of the
proliferating manuals that proclaimed the new science of domestic
economy. She seemed to realize that she had novel problems which
required new solutions.

One of the clearest illustrations of the middle-class woman's
willingness to participate in the mainstream of modern society was her
acceptance of innovation and technology into her home. The sewing
machine is one very important example. Objections were voiced
concerning the sewing machine, similar in many ways to the objections
roused early in the century over the introduction of machines into
industry. There was a lament that the sewing machines would destroy

the long-valued skill of hand sewing — that element of personal touch associated with the craft and womanhood. However, the criticism was never persuasive enough to deter the middle-class woman as she readily adopted this new invention and eagerly sought information on it. No doubt the primary reason women welcomed this advance in technology was necessity. There were just so many hours in the day, and so much time to spend on sewing. With the sewing machine, the middle-class woman was able efficiently and economically to come to terms with both problems. However, one cannot neglect the fact that she was willing to give up, almost overnight, a long tradition of hand sewing in favor of a machine which did take away much of the personal touch. One could further suggest that the sewing machine was, in some ways, an expression of the woman's growing sense of individualism within the household. In buying the machine she acquired a new piece of property that was hers, as well as one that worked primarily to her own benefit. This does not mean that she was the heroine of passive consumerism as depicted in the conventional image — the manifestation of the paraphernalia of gentility — but in her own sphere she was trying to define herself, as well as make her life easier, in new ways.

Viewed in the light of modernization, the familiar list of other household innovations that gained ground in the later nineteenth century assumes new importance. One could argue that if the middle-class woman had not been so receptive to innovation, the process of modernization, which depended on mechanization, could not have progressed as rapidly as it did. As was noted in the earlier discussion of the mistress of the house, the middle-class woman was the prime consumer of many of the new products of industrialization. She was the only woman who both needed and could afford the advances in technology. The upper-class woman with her retinue of servants did not necessarily need the innovations, while the working-class women could not afford them. Other major industries, such as advertising and women's magazines, depended heavily on the middle-class woman as consumer. In other words, because of her new attitudes and her decision-making power, the middle-class woman emerged as a significant force for consumer-related economic development.

There are other aspects of the process of modernization in the life of the middle-class woman which are not as easy to recognize but equally significant. In the discussion on health it was shown that the middle-class woman was intimately involved with many of the changing attitudes now associated with modernization, such as sanitation. Also, the middle-class woman more and more rejected the traditional, fatalistic attitude toward death, especially where infant and maternal mortality were concerned. By seeking advice about her health and that of her children, she demonstrated the belief that her world could be ordered

150

and improved. She expressed a growing reliance on science; first through her purchase of health manuals which were generally written by doctors, and second by her increasing use of doctors to tend to her health problems. There was some evidence that she clung more to traditional ways in this particular aspect of her life than as mistress of the house. The reliance on quack medicines was certainly based to a great extent on tradition, but we have noted that the key to success for many of the patent medicines in the nineteenth century was the claim to innovation and scientific expertise, most often in the forms of bogus testimonials from doctors. It was also pointed out that one major reason for apparently tradionalist behavior lay with the reluctance of the medical profession to implement available innovations rather than with the woman.

The Victorian woman's personal life was profoundly altered by modernization. This was seen very clearly in her receptiveness to chloroform, artificial feeding and contraceptive devices. In all three cases, especially the last, there was evidence of the middle-class woman's growing desire to order her own personal comfort, thereby demonstrating a sense of strong personal autonomy. In the discussion of contraception the development of a modern mentality was most evident. Women accepted contraceptive devices for selfish reasons in part, to insure their own physical well-being by limiting the number of children they bore, and to increase their opportunities for sexual pleasure and gratification.

There were, of course, ambiguities in 'modern' attitudes themselves. For example, the woman's desire for greater personal autonomy was juxtaposed with the equally modern notion that as mother she should devote herself intensively to the care and attention of her child. This is a dilemma in the modernization of women that has even yet to be resolved. And these and other modern attitudes did not win complete acceptance by the 1870s, for the hold of traditional values was still strong. The period covered in this study emerges as an important transitional stage. The advent of birth control is perhaps the most obvious sign of the development of new attitudes, and by releasing some energies from traditional functions it sets the stage for other developments.[15] But we can now see that this change was part of a larger modernization package, which saw the middle-class woman seeking to define herself, albeit within the family, as an individual and to gain new control over her body.

The changes in behavior and outlook that did occur in this transitional period were both marked and confused by the constant carping from contemporary publicists, which has in turn tended to mislead historians dealing with Victorian women. Contemporary observers found the middle-class woman a convenient vehicle for criticism of modernity generally. They sensed her desire for new things and therefore exaggerated her indulgence in luxuries. Many critics, some of the strongest of which came from among the religious spokesmen, found an audience among middle-class women themselves. This undoubtedly reflected an uncertainty among many of these women about the new ways, even as they largely persisted in them. There was also some unintended coincidence involved: reading matter that was sought primarily for recipes or patterns often contained a lament over the decline of true womanhood. And this raises again the question of the impact of the criticism in heightening the middle-class woman's sense of insecurity and anxiety. Victorian society, in terms of its official culture, was very demanding of its women. It expected them to be perfect ladies, perfect wives, and perfect mothers. The Victorian woman was to have an observing eye, a calculating head, a skilful hand, concise speech, a gentle step, external tidiness and internal purity. She was expected to exercise constant patience and forebearance, in spite of narrow means, inconvenient houses, crying children and preoccupied husbands. Her responsibilities were indeed overwhelming, and if she failed she had only herself to blame:

> ... on you *fair* and amiable creature who was born to
> assuage our sufferings, dispel care, wipe away the tears of
> grief, and to exalt all our enjoyments, much more depends
> than you commonly imagine. For, if we so frequently
> remark that marriages of attachment end in anything but
> cordiality and happiness, – if it be obvious that indifference
> has crept in where all was once love and respect, – it is (we
> are sorry to state) but too probable that the lady has
> originated this fearful change. The angel has become a demon
> of domestic strife.[16]

To be sure, middle-class men encountered some criticism of their life style as well, but it was never as intense as that directed against women. For women, the adverse public culture could not only cause feelings of guilt about new patterns of behavior but could inhibit a consciousness of the significance of this behavior. Women were seeking more autonomy and control but they may not fully have realized their own goals, because they lacked public sanction. Here is another complicating factor that requires consideration in an understanding of the modernization of women.

Clearly, the middle class needs renewed attention if we are to grasp the dynamics of change in nineteenth-century Britain, and indeed elsewhere. The study of Victorian women suggests that the middle class had not only its own life style but a complex series of problems that have rarely been appreciated in the cursory treatment the class has received from historians. Its men have been too often dismissed as exploiters or conquerors;[17] its women as useless ornaments barely deserving a serious history. In fact, while the social historian cannot point to the stark misery that has lent drama to many of the treatments of the working class, the problems with which the middle class was grappling have at least as much enduring significance. Aspirations were often unmet in a life that remained rigorous in many ways. The class did advance, and Victorian women did benefit from the modernization process. But the changes were hard-won, for new ideas were the product neither of leisure nor of luxury. Most middle-class women had enough margin to avoid taking refuge in traditional family functions alone, but they suffered considerable anxiety as they tried to develop a new life style. That many of the behavior patterns they developed ultimately became part of the modernization of women more generally is a tribute to their ingenuity as well as their influence. But the complexities of the transitional period have enduring significance as well, for they have by no means been shaken off. Here is where middle-class women, like the middle class as a whole, deserve a careful historical assessment, and not merely a characterization.

Notes

1. Ester Boserup, *Women and Economic Modernization* (London, 1970).
2. Alex Inkeles, 'The Modernization of Man,' in Myron Weiner (ed.), *Modernization: The Dynamics of Growth* (New York, 1966)
3. Stearns, 'Working-Class Women.'
4. Anderson, *Family Structure.*
5. Beeton, *Household Management*, p.19.
6. Briggs, *Modern England*, p. 465.
7. Perkin, *Origins of English Society*, pp. 199-200.
8. *The Englishwoman's Domestic Magazine*, Vol. III, p. 95.
9. Ibid., Vol. XVIII, (1870), pp. 37-8.
10. *The New Home: Or Wedded Life, Its Duties, Cares, and Pleasures* (by the author of A Woman's Secret), 3rd Ed. (London, 1862), p. 84.
11. Dr. John Hadden, 'Intemperance in Women, with Special Reference to its Effect on the Reproductive System,' in *The British Medical Journal* (21 August 1875), p. 232.
12. Dr. Robert Dick, *The Connexion of Health and Beauty or the Dependence of a Pleasing Face and Figure on Physical Intellectual, and Moral Religion* (London, 1857), p. 31.
13. Ibid., p. 28.
14. Ibid., p. 32.
15. See Shorter's article, 'Female Emancipation.'
16. *Economy for the Single and Married*, p. 37.

APPENDIX

CAMBERWELL AS A MIDDLE-CLASS SUBURB, 1851-1871

Identifying a residential unit as middle-class, in the terms used by census-takers or the recorders of vital statistics, is not a neat task. The easiest way to trace middle-class family patterns, through the occupationally-identified birth, death and marriage records housed in Somerset House, is blocked by the policies of the Registrar-General's office, for this agency does not regard itself as an archive or even, in the words of one of its representatives, as an agency serving the public at all. Hence for purposes of this study the only recourse was to a community identifiably more middle-class than most, through the censuses, and this turned the research almost inevitably to a London suburb.

Camberwell has been admirably studied by H.J. Dyos. From the standpoint of conventional urban history it long remained a middle-class suburb, emerging from an agricultural adjunct of the city by mid-century. Its ratio of inhabited houses per capita, for example, stood distinctly higher than that of London; in 1871 there were 17 per cent as many inhabited houses as people, compared to 13 per cent in the city as a whole. This was a rapidly growing suburb, expanding by 31 per cent between 1851 and 1861 and 56 per cent during the next decade (compared to overall city growth of 19 and 16 per cent respectively). Oddly, however, while Dyos clearly labels Camberwell a middle-class suburb well beyond this period, his book did not utilize the occupational census materials that, lacking tax records would best substantiate such a claim.

Camberwell data can unfortunately be found only beginning with the 1861 census. At this point the suburb had clearly attracted a disproportionate number of professionals: 10.5 per cent of the employed males, compared to 6.9 per cent for the whole of London. It had a less sharp edge in the formal commerce categories, 10.8 per cent to 7.3 per cent. Overall, including identifiable agents or owners in other operations (coal deliveries, textiles and dress) Camberwell's male middle class was at least 35 per cent of the total in 1861, compared to 19 per cent for the city as a whole. This statistical difference is great enough to be reflected in birth and death statistics, even though it falls short of making Camberwell a perfect middle-class model. There was relatedly an unusually low percentage of labourers (5.5 per cent) and transport workers (7.5 per cent); in other words, those males who were not middle-class were most likely to be artisans, although agriculture commanded over 5 per cent of the male population (compared to 2 per cent for London as a whole).

In 1871 the professional edge had been lost. Camberwell and London were both about 10 per cent professional, of the adult male total. But the advantage in commerce was still more pronounced; in outright commerce Camberwell had 12 per cent to London's 8 per cent, and in the broader commercial category (Category III of the census) Camberwell was up to 21 per cent. Overall the middle class was now at least 42 per cent of Camberwell's employed male population, compared to 26 per cent for London as a whole. In other categories Camberwell was 23 per cent artisanal (compared to 22 per cent for London), 8 per cent laborer (to 10 per cent), 9 per cent transport (to 12 per cent) and so on. Again, not so clear a middle-class dominance as to make the vital statistics definitely indicative of middle-class patterns, but close enough for high probability.

The probability is heightened by the census description of women. In 1861 49 per cent of the Camberwell adult female population were housewives and non-employed female relations. This was actually under the London total of 56 per cent. But by 1871 the middle-class pattern was decisive; 64 per cent for Camberwell, with London down to 54 per cent. The same differential held as to servants. Camberwell had but 17 per cent of its female population servants in 1861, compared to 23 per cent for the whole city. But 10 per cent of the population were general servants, compared to 8 per cent for the city, 5 per cent 'other' servants (to 4 per cent) and only 1 per cent charwomen (to 10 per cent). Camberwell thus had only a slight margin in the rich households that could afford more than a general servant — this probably reflected the importance of professional men as heads of households in 1861 — but a more substantial one-servant class. It is also true that there were fewer servants than middle-class heads of household, which meant either a servantless young family or the importation of chars who could not afford to live in Camberwell itself. In 1871 the overall female servant percentage had declined in both London and Camberwell, but much more slightly in the latter: to 15 per cent compared to London's 18 per cent. In both census years Camberwell attracted an unusual number of female home owners (probably artisanal boarding house keepers), dressmakers, laundresses and the like. In other words, as with males, Camberwell had a large middle-class minority and a large artisanal minority, which was drawn in part to serve the middle class; servants aside, it had disproportionately few lower-class elements. So, although again the diversity of the female population prevents neat generalizations, the occupational evidence suggests a distinct difference from London as a whole, sufficiently marked to show in the vital statistics.

And on that last point, a final bit of census data: 0.4 per cent of

Camberwell's employed male population consisted of physicians in 1861, compared to 0.06 per cent in London. Camberwell lagged slightly in dentists but had twice the per capita number of druggists. On the other hand, Camberwell, with 0.0002 per cent of its adult female population composed of midwives (a third of the London rate) had fewer of the more traditional health practitioners. It is clear that the new middle-class community was attracting its medical counterpart, which makes the vital statistics all the more significant.

SELECTED BIBLIOGRAPHY

The problem of sources and their representativeness remains considerable for the social historian of women. More intensive studies of quantitative data are definitely needed, as noted throughout this study, The type of sources listed below naturally limits the permissible amount of inference. As an example — though one which defies quantification, unlike the discussions of disease or demographic change — one cannot infer that female sexual pleasure was actually heightened simply because it was encouraged in many marriage manuals. Overall it is difficult to posit certainties. However, a large sampling of marriage manuals over a period of time can indicate important changes, even though there is need for further investigation. One must not lose sight of the fact that we are only at the beginning of studying the history of women as an element of social history.

PRIMARY SOURCES

Books

Acton, William. *The Functions and Disorders of the Reproductive Organs in Childhood, Youth, Adult Age and Advanced Life, Considered in Their Physiological, Social, and Moral Relations.* London, 1862

Allbutt, Henry Albert, M.D. *Every Mother's Handbook: A Guide to the Management of Her Children from Birth Through Infancy and Childhood with Instructions for Preliminary Treatment of Accidents and Illness.* London, 1897
The Wife's Handbook: *How A Woman Should Order Herself During Pregnancy in the Lying-In Room and After Delivery, With Hints on the Management of the Baby, and Other Matters of Importance, Necessary to be Known by Married Women.* London, 1886

Ansell, C. *On the Rate of Mortality at Early Periods of Life, the Age at Marriage, the Number of Children to a Marriage, the Length of a Generation, and Other Statistics of Families in the Upper and Professional Classes.* 1874.

Armstrong, John. *The Young Woman's Guide to Virtue, Economy and Happiness.* Newcastle Upon Tyne, 1817

Ashwell, Samuel, M.D. *A Practical Treatise on the Diseases Peculiar to Women.* London, 1844.

Baxter, R.D. *National Income.* London, 1868

Beauty is Power. London, 1871.

Beeton, Isabella. *The Book of Household Management.* London, 1861.

Belloc, Bessie Rayner Parker. *Essay on Woman's Work.* 2nd ed. London, 1865.

Blackwell, Elizabeth, M.D. *Counsel to Parents on the Moral Education of their Children.* London, 1878.
How to Keep a Household in Health. London, 1870.
The Human Element in Sex: Being a Medical Enquiry into the Relationship of Sexual Physiology to Christian Mortality. 2nd ed. London, 1896

Booth, Charles. *Life and Labour of the People in London*, Vol. VIII. London, 1896.

Bull, Thomas, M.D. *Hints to Mothers, for the Management of Health, During the Period of Pregnancy, and Lying-In Room; with an Exposure of Popular Errors in Connection with Those Subjects.* London, 1837.

Carlile, Richard. *Every Woman's Book; or What is Love?* 2nd ed. London, 1826.

Carter, Robert Brudenell. *On the Pathology and Treatment of Hysteria.*

London, 1853.

Charasse, Pye Henry. *Advice to a Wife on the Management of Her Own Health*, London, 1842.

Churchill, Fleetwood, M.D. *On the Diseases of Women: Including Those of Pregnancy and Childbed.* Philadelphia, 1857.

Colquhoun, Patrick. *A Treatise on Indigence.* 1806.

Conquest, J.T. M.D. *Letter to a Mother on the Management of Herself and Her Children in Health and Diseases, Embracing the Subject of Pregnancy, Childbirth, Nursing, Food, Exercise, Bathing, Clothing, Etc., Etc.; With Remarks on Chloroform.* London, 1848.

Dick, Robert, M.D. *The Connexion of Health and Beauty on the Dependence of a Pleasing Face and Figure on Physical Intellectual, and Moral Religion.* London, 1857.

Domestic Servants as They Are and As They Ought To Be (By a Practical Mistress of a Household). Brighton, 1859.

(Drysdale, George). *The Elements of Social Science; or Physical Sexual and Natural Religion. An Exposition of the True Cause and Only Cure of the Three Primary Social Evils: Poverty, Prostitution, and Celibacy.* By a Doctor of Medicine. London, 1854.

Economy for the Single and Married; or The Young Wife and Bachelor's Guide to Income and Expenditure on 50 Pounds Per Annum, 100 Pounds Per Annum, 150 Per Annum, 200 Pounds Per Annum; With Estimates Up to 500 Pounds Per Annum. 1845.

Ellis, Sarah Stickney. *The Daughters of England.* London, 1843.
The Mothers of England. London, 1845.
The Wives of England. London, 1843.
The Women of England, Their Social Duties and Domestic Habits. London, 1839.

The English Matron. (By the Author of the English Gentlewoman). London, 1846.

Farr, William. *Vital Statistics.* London, 1885.

Fennings, Alfred, M.D. *Every Mother's Book; or the Child's Best Doctor.* West Cowes, 1856.

Gordon, Alexander, M.D. 'A Treatise on the Epidemic Puerperal Fever of Aberdeen 1795,' in Walter Radcliffe, *Milestones in Midwifery.*

The Handbook of Women's Work. Edited by L.M.H. London, 1876.

Health and Home. (By a Quiet Woman). London, 1875.

Holyoake, Austin. *Large or Small Families: On Which Side Lies the Balance of Comfort?* London, 1870.

Home Difficulties; Or, Whose Fault Is It? A Few Words on the Servant Question. By the Author of 'A Woman's Secrets.' London, 1866.

The Household: A Book of Reference Upon Subjects Related to Domestic Economy and Home Enjoyment. London, 1866.

James, Emily, ed. *Englishwoman's Year Book and Directory, 1899-1900.*

London, 1900.

Kerr, Alice, M.D. 'Lectures to Women,' *Womanhood*. No. 3. Manchester, 1884.

Knowlton, Charles. *Fruits of Philosophy; Or, the Private Companion of Young Married Couples*. London, 1833.

Linton, E. Lynn. *The Girl of the Period, and Other Social Essays*. Vols. I & II. London, 1883.

Mason, S. *The Philosophy of Female Health: Being an Enquiry Into Its Connextions; With Observations on the Nature, Causes and Treatment of Female Disorders in General*. London, 1845.

The Mothers' Home-Book: A Book for Her Own and Her Children's Management with Hints and Helps for Every-Day Emergencies. London, 1879.

The Mother's Medical Adviser. London, 1843.

The New Home: Or Wedded Life, Its Duties, Cares and Pleasures. By the Author of 'A Woman's Secret.' 3rd. ed. London, 1862.

A New System of Practical Domestic Economy Founded on Modern Discoveries and the Private Communications of Persons of Experience. 3rd ed. London, 1828.

Owen, Robert Dale. *Moral Physiology; Or a Brief and Plain Treatise on the Population Question*. New York, 1831.

Place, Francis. *To the Married of Both Sexes in Genteel Life*. 1823. Place Collection, British Museum, Vol. LXI, Part II.

Ryan, Michael, M.D. *The Philosophy of Marriage, in Its Social, Moral, and Physical Relations With an Account of the Diseases of the Genita-Urinary Organs which Impair or Destroy the Reproductive Function, and Induce a Variety of Complaints; With the Physiology of Generations on the Vegetable and Animal Kingdom; Being Part of a Course of Obstetric Lectures Delivered at the North London School of Medicine*. London, 1837.

Sauerbeck, Augustus. *Prices of Commodities During the Last Seven Years*. London, 1893.

Simpson, James Y., M.D. 'An Account of a New Anaesthetic Agent, As a Substitute for Sulphuric Ether in Surgery and Midwifery.' 1848, in Walter Radcliffe, *Milestones in Midwifery*. Bristol, 1967.

Soyer, Alexis, *The Modern Housewife or Ménagère*. New York, 1849.

Tilt, Edward John, M.D. *The Elements of Health, and Principles of Female Hygiene*. London, 1852.

Walsh, John. *A Manual of Domestic Economy: Suited to Families Spending from 100 Pounds to 1000 Pounds a Year*. London, 1853. *A Manual of Domestic Economy: Suited to Families Spending from 150 Pounds to 1500 Pounds a Year*. London, 1874.

Ward and Lock's Home Book, A Domestic Cyclopaedia. London, 1880.

Warren, Eliza. *Comfort for Small Incomes*. London, 1866.

How I Managed My Children From Infancy to Marriage. London, 1865.

How I Managed My House on Two Hundred Pounds a Year. London, 1865.

Weatherly, Lionel, M.D. *The Young Wife's Own Book: A Manual of Personal and Family Hygiene, Containing Everything that the Young Wife and Mother Ought to Know Concerning Her Own Health and That of Her Children at the Most Important Periods of Life.* London, 1882.

Webster, T. *An Encyclopaedia of Domestic Economy, Comprising Such Subjects as are Most Immediately Connected with Housekeeping.* New York, 1845.

White, Charles, M.D. A Treatise on the Management of Pregnant and *Lying-In Women,* quoted in Walter Radcliffe *Milestones in Midwifery.* Bristol, 1967.

'The Age at Which Child-Bearing Ceases.' *The British Medical Journal,* 6 February 1875.

Articles

Allbutt, Henry Albert, M.D. 'Evil Produced by Over-Bearing and Excessive Lactation,' *Malthusian Tract No. 4.,* n.d.
'Answer to a Young Mother's Queries — Obedience a Habit — Obedience a Virtue,' *The British Mothers' Magazine,* Vol. V, June, 1849.

Bakewell, R. Hall, M.D. 'Infant Mortality, and Its Causes,' *The British Mothers' Journal,* June-December 1857.

Greg, W.R., 'Life at High Pressure,' *The Contemporary Review,* March 1875 Hadden, John, M.D. 'Intemperance in Women, With Special Reference to its Effect on the Reproductive System,' *The British Medical Journal,* 21 August 1875.

'How To Manage a Baby,' *The British Mothers' Journal,* June 1858.

'The Ill-Health of Women,' *The Mothers' Companion,* Vol. II, 1880

Kidd, Charles, 'On Chloroform and Some of Its Clinical Uses,' *The London Medical Review or Monthly Journal of Medical and Surgical Science,* Vol. II, July 1861 — June 1962.

Lankester, E., M.D. 'Plain Rules for the Management of Infants,' *The London Medical Record,* 4 March 1874.

Moore, T.V. Rev., 'The Family as Government,' *The British Mothers' Journal,* May 1856.

Morris, Joseph, M.D., 'The Use of Soothing Syrups,' *The British Medical Journal,* Vol. II, 30 October 1875.

'A New Food for Infants,' *The Englishwoman's Domestic Magazine,* Vol. VI, April 1869

'On the Importance of Parental Consistency and Cooperation,' *The British Mothers' Journal for 1857*, June 1857.

'On the Use of Night-Caps — Seven Years Experience of the Practicability of Limiting the Number of a Family, by the Best Known Methods; Including Some Valuable and Novel Information, Never Before Published; Addressed Exclusively to Married Couples by a Married Man (with Six Children),' quoted in Peter Fryer, *The Man of Pleasure's Companion: A Nineteenth Century Anthology of Amorous Entertainment.* London, 1965.

'Parental Submission,' *The British Mothers' Family Magazine for 1864*, July 1864.

'Physics and Infancy,' *The Family Economist*, Vol. I, 1848.

'Women in Domestic Life,' *Magazine of Domestic Economy*, Vol. I, 1835-6.

Periodicals

Annual Register.

The British Medical Journal.

The British Mothers' Magazine. Vol. 1-11. London, 1845-55.
Continued as *The British Mothers' Journal.* London, 1856-63.
The British Mothers' Family Magazine for 1864. London, 1864.

The Englishwoman's Domestic Magazine.

The Englishwoman's Journal.

The Family Economist.

The Family Friend.

The Ladies Journal — A Newspaper of Fashion, Literature, Music and Variety. 1847.

London Illustrated News.

The London Medical Review. Vol. III, No. 111. September 1862.

The Magazine of Domestic Economy. Vol. I. London, 1835-6.

The Mother's Companion. London, 1890.

The Mother's Friend: A Monthly Magazine. London, 1848-95.

The Queen.

Whitaker's Almanac.

Government Documents

Annual Report of the Registrar General of Births, Deaths, and Marriages in England. 1848-87.

Census of England and Wales, 1871.

Census of England and Wales, 1891.

England: Causes of the 420,977 Deaths Registered in the Year 1847. London, 1851.

162

Fifth Annual Report of the Registrar General of Births, Deaths, and Marriages in England. London, 1843.

'Report on the Fertility of Marriage,' Vol. XIII. *Census of England and Wales.* 1911.

Report from the Select Committee on Midwives Registration. Vol. XIV, Part I. June 1892.

SECONDARY SOURCES

Books

Anderson, Michael. *Family Structure in Nineteenth Century Lancashire.* Cambridge, 1971.

Armstrong, Alan. *Stability and Change in an English Country Town. A Social Study of York 1801-51.* Cambridge 1974.

Banks, J.A. *Prosperity and Parenthood.* London, 1954.
and Banks, Olive. *Feminism and Family Planning in Victorian England.* New York, 1964.

Barnard, H.C. *A History of English Education from 1760.* London, 1961.

Best, Geoffrey. *Mid-Victorian Britain 1851-1875.* London, 1971.

Boserup, Ester. *Women and Economic Modernization.* London, 1970.

Briggs, Asa. *The Making of Modern England 1783-1867.* New York, 1959.

Burton, Elizabeth. *The Pageant of Early Victory England.* New York, 1972.

Checkland, S.G. *The Rise of Industrial Society in England 1865-85.* London, 1964.

Cobbold, Helen M. *Statistical Analysis of Infant Mortality and Its Causes in the United Kingdom.* London, 1910.

Crow, Duncan. *The Victorian Woman.* New York, 1971.

Cunnington, C.W. *Feminine Attitudes in the Nineteenth Century.* London, 1935.

Davidoff, Leonore. *The Employment of Married Women in England.* Unpublished M.A. Thesis University of London, 1956.

Daumard, Adeline. *La Bourgeoisie Parisienne de 1815 à 1848.* Paris, 1963.

Dunbar, Janet. *The Early Victorian Woman, Some Aspects of Her Life 1837-57.* London, 1957.

Forster, John. *Class Struggle in the Industrial Revolution.* London, 1974.

Fryer, Peter. *The Birth Controllers.* London, 1965.

Gathorne-Hardy, Jonathan. *The Rise and Fall of the British Nanny.*

London, 1972.

Graham, Harry. *Eternal Eve: The Mysteries of Birth and the Customs that Surround it.* London, 1960.

Green, Shirley. *The Curious History of Contraception.* London, 1971.

Harrison, J.F.C. *The Early Victorians 1832-51.* London, 1971.

Hewitt, Margaret, *Wives and Mothers in Victorian Industry.* London, 1958.

Himes, Norman E. *Medical History of Contraception.* New York, 1936.

Innes, John W. *Class Fertility Trends in England and Wales 1876-1934.* Princeton, 1938.

Kamm, Josephine. *Hope Deferred: Girls' Education in English History.* London, 1965.

Lambert-Dansette, Jean. *Quelques Familles Du Patronat Textile De Lille-Armentières.* Lille, 1954.

Laslett, Peter. *The World We have Lost.* New York, 1960.

Lewis, Roy and Angus Maude, Edmund Upton, *The English Middle Classes.* London, 1949.

Lockwood, David. *The Blackcoated Worker; A Study in Class Consciousness.* London, 1966.

Loesser, Arthur. *Men, Women and Pianos: A Social History.* New York, 1954.

McGregor, O.R. *Divorce in England, a Centenary Study.* London, 1957.

Moraze, Charles. *La France Bourgeoisie.* Paris, 1952.
The Triumph of the Middle Class, A Study of European Values in the Nineteenth Century. Cleveland, 1966.

Musgrove, P.W. *Society and Education in England Since 1800.* London, 1968.

Nef, Wanda F. *Victorian Working Women.* London, 1929.

O'Neill, William. *The Woman Movement: Feminism in the United States and England.* Chicago, 1969.

Osborne, John W. *The Silent Revolution.* New York, 1970.

Pearsall, R. *The Worm in the Bud: The World of Victorian Sexuality.* New York, 1969.

Perkin, Harold. *The Origins of Modern English Society 1780-1880.* London, 1969.

Pinchbeck, Ivy. *Women Workers in the Industrial Revolution.* London, 1930.

Poynter, F.N.L., ed. *The Evolution of Medical Practice in Britain.* London, 1961.

Radcliffe, Walter. *Milestones in Midwifery.* Bristol, 1967.

Report of the Royal Commission on Population. Vol. XIX, 1948-9.

Ricci, James V. *One Hundred Years of Gynaecology 1800-1900.* Philadelphia, 1945.

Simon, Brian. *Studies in the History of Education, 1780-1870.* London, 1960.

Stenton, Doris Mary. *The English Woman in History.* London, 1957.

Thompson, F.N.L. *Hampstead: Building a Borough 1650-65.* Boston, 1974.

Thomson, Patricia. *The Victorian Heroine, A Changing Ideal 1837-73.* London, 1956.

Vicinus, Martha, ed. *Suffer and Be Still: Women in the Victorian Age.* Bloomington, 1972.

Wood, Clive and Suitters, Beryl. *The Fight for Acceptance: A History of Contraception.* Aylesbury, 1970.

ARTICLES

Cominos, Peter T., 'Innocent Femina Sensualise in Unconscious Conflict.' *Suffer and Be Still.* In Martha Vicinus, ed. Bloomington, 1972.

Degler, Carl N., 'What Ought To Be and What Was: Women's Sexuality in the Nineteenth Century,' *American Historical Review,* Vol. 79, No. 5, December 1974.

Glass, D.V., 'Population and Population Movements in England and Wales 1700-1850.' In *Population and Population Movements in England and Wales 1700 to 1850.* D.V. Glass, ed. New York, 1967.

Hobsbawm, Eric, 'The Labour Aristocracy in Nineteenth-Century Britain.' In *Labouring Men.* New York, 1967.

Hollingsworth, J.H., 'A Demographic Study of the British Ducal Families.' In *Population in History: Essays in Historical Demography.* D.V. Glass and D.E.C. Eversley. London, 1965.

Inkeles, Alex, 'The Modernization of Man.' In *Modernization: The Dynamics of Growth.* Myron Weiner, ed. New York, 1966.

McBride, Theresa, 'Social Mobility for the Lower Class: Domestic Servants in France, *Journal of Social History,* Vol. 8, No. 1, September 1974.

Neale, R.S., 'Class and Class-Consciousness in Early Nineteenth-Century England: Three Classes or Five?' *Victorian Studies,* Vol. XII, September 1968.

Neuman, R.P., 'Masturbation, Madness and the Modern Concepts of Childhood and Adolescene,' *Journal of Social History,* March 1975.

Newsholme, A and Stevenson, T.H.C., 'The Decline of Human Fertility in the United Kingdom and Other Countries as Shown by Corrected Birth Rates, *Journal of the Royal Statistical Society.* Vol. LXIX, 1906.

Peel, John, 'The Manufacture and Retailing of Contraception in

England, *Population Studies,* Vol. XVII, 1963.

Peterson, M. Jeanne, 'The Victorian Governess: Status Incongruence in Family and Society,' *Victorian Studies,* Vol. XIV, No. 1.

Shorter, Edward' 'Female Emancipation, Birth Control and Fertility in European History,' *American Historical Review,* Vol. 78, No. 3, June, 1973.

Wells, Robert V., 'Family History and Demographic Transition,' *Journal of Social History.* Vol. 9, No. 1.

Stearns, Peter N., 'Working-Class Women in Britain, 1890-1914.' In *Suffer and Be Still.* Martha Vicinus, ed. Bloomington, 1972.

Wood, Ann, 'The Fashionable Diseases: Women's Complaints and their Treatment in Nineteenth-Century America,' *Journal of Interdisciplinary History,* Vol. 3, 1973.

Wood, George H., 'Real Wages and the Standard of Comfort Since 1850,' *Journal of the Royal Statistical Society,* Vol. LXXII, March 1909.

INDEX

mortality in, 98
London Maternal Association, 76
Lower middle class, income of, 45

Manual of Domestic Economy, 13, 47, 51
Marriage: manuals, 124, 128, 138; patterns, 1, 2, 3, 4, 5; Victorians' view of, 123-4, 128
Married Woman's Property Act (1870), 9
Masturbation, 126, 129
Maternal mortality, 62, 76, 95; birth control and, 114; puerperal fever cause of, 86, 87; statistics, 81, 82
Matrimonial Cause Act (1857), 8-9
Medical History of Contraception, 115
Menstrual disorders, 71-2
Middle class: definition of, 17, 18, 38, 39, 41, 43, 45; expension of, 2; income patterns, 39-45, 55
Midwives: criticism of, 79; numbers, registration and training, 79, 80, 156
Modern Housewife of Ménagère, 13
Modernization, impact on Victorian woman, 1, 2, 114, 120, 144-53
Moral Education, 126
Morris, Dr Joseph, 106, 107
Morrison, James, 'The Hygeist', 67
Motherhood, and the Victorian woman, 74-90, 148
Mother's Medical Adviser, 102
Mothers of England, 13
Mrs Winslow's Soothing Syrup, 106

National Income, 43, 44
Nef, Wanda F., 9
New Home; or Wedded Life, 148
New System of Practical Domestic Economy, 40
Newsholme, A., 115

Obstetrics, 63, 71, 77, 78, 79, 80, 81, 83; use of chloroform in, 84, 85, 86
On the Diseases of Women, 63
Opium: use in childbirth, 85; taken by children, 106, 107; taken by women, 149
Ould, ––, 85
Ovariotomies, 64, 72

Pasteur, Louis, 94
Patent (quack) medicines, 67, 68, 106, 107, 151
Pearsall, R., 5
Periodicals and magazines:
    British Medical Journal, 76, 148
    British Mothers' Journal, 95, 99, 102
    British Mothers' Magazine, 76, 147
    Englishwoman's Domestic Magazine (EDM), 14, 24, 29, 40, 46, 51, 103, 110, 147, 148
    Family Friend, 14, 110
    Female Friend, 128
    Housekeeper's Magazine, 24
    London Illustrated News, 52
    London Medical Review, 85, 125
    Magazine of Domestic Economy, 30, 76
    Mother's Companion, 53
    Mother's Friend, 76, 96
    Saturday Review, 23
Pessaries, 64, 133, 135, 136, 138
Pianos, 52, 53
Pinchbeck, Ivy, 9
Place, Francis, and birth control, 131, 132
Population question, and birth rate, 114
Poverty, and birth control, 115
Pregnancy; 65, 74; determination of, 68, 71, 82, 83, 84, 93; discussion of, 75, 89, 146; frequency of, 77, 122; among servant girls, 90; warnings on, 82, 84
Pre-natal care, 82, 84
Prosperity and Parenthood, 15, 116
Puerperal fever, 82, 86, 87, 89, 93, 94

Ramsbottom, Francis, 84
Reading material, of women, 147, 152
Registrar General, Annual Reports, 78-9, 96, 104
Religious decline, among women, 146-7
Rent, in household budget, 28, 48, 50
Rentoul, Dr, 80
Report of the Royal Commission on Population, 115